SAMMY SOSA

OVERCOMING ADVERSITY

SAMMY SOSA

Ann G. Gaines

Introduction by James Scott Brady,
Trustee, the Center to Prevent Handgun Violence
Vice Chairman, the Brain Injury Foundation

Chelsea House Publishers
Philadelphia

Frontis: *Sammy Sosa is carried by teammates after hitting his 61st and 62nd home runs of the 1998 season on September 13. The Chicago slugger, who grew up poor and malnourished in the Dominican Republic, has become one of the game's best players.*

Cover Photo: AP Photo/Jason Wise; Background: Corbis/Reinhard Eisele; Back: David Durochik/SportsPics © 1998

CHELSEA HOUSE PUBLISHERS

EDITOR IN CHIEF Stephen Reginald
PRODUCTION MANAGER Pamela Loos
ART DIRECTOR Sara Davis
DIRECTOR OF PHOTOGRAPHY Judy L. Hasday
MANAGING EDITOR James D. Gallagher
SENIOR PRODUCTION EDITOR J. Christopher Higgins

Staff for **SAMMY SOSA**
ASSOCIATE ART DIRECTOR Takeshi Takahashi
DESIGNER Keith Trego
PICTURE RESEARCHER Sandy Jones

© 2000 by Chelsea House Publishers, a subsidiary of Haights Cross Communications. All rights reserved. Printed and bound in the United States of America.

The Chelsea House World Wide Web site address is: www.chelseahouse.com

First Printing

1 3 5 7 9 8 6 4 2

Library of Congress Cataloging-in-Publication Data

Gaines, Ann G.
Sammy Sosa / Ann Gaines.

p. cm. — (Overcoming adversity)
Includes bibliographical references and index.
Summary: A biography of the Chicago Cubs outfielder who in 1998, along with Mark McGuire, broke the home run record previously set by Roger Maris.

ISBN 0-7910-5300-8 (hardcover). — ISBN 0-7910-5301-6 (pbk.)
1. Sosa, Sammy, 1968– Juvenile literature. 2. Baseball players—Dominican Republic—Biography—Juvenile literature. [1. Sosa, Sammy, 1968– 2. Baseball players] I. Title. II. Series
GV865.S59G35   1999
796.357'092—dc21   99–34135
[B]   CIP

CONTENTS

	On Facing Adversity *James Scott Brady*	7
1	THE 60–60 CLUB	11
2	HUMBLE BEGINNINGS	17
3	A TEEN IN THE MINOR LEAGUES	25
4	MAKING IT IN THE MAJORS	35
5	BECOMING A STAR	43
6	LEARNING TO BE PATIENT	53
7	ENTERING THE RACE	59
8	MOST VALUABLE PLAYER	65
9	A HELPING HAND	75
10	BACK IN THE GROOVE	81

Chronology	88
Appendix: Charitable Foundations	90
Appendix: Sammy Sosa's Baseball Statistics	93
Appendix: Babe Ruth	95
Appendix: The 1961 Home-Run Race	99
Further Reading	102
Index	104

OVERCOMING ADVERSITY

TIM ALLEN
comedian/performer

MAYA ANGELOU
author

APOLLO 13 MISSION
astronauts

LANCE ARMSTRONG
professional cyclist

DREW BARRYMORE
actress

JAMES BRADY
gun control activist

DREW CAREY
comedian/performer

JIM CARREY
comedian/performer

BILL CLINTON
U.S. president

TOM CRUISE
actor

MICHAEL J. FOX
actor

WHOOPI GOLDBERG
comedian/performer

EKATERINA GORDEEVA
figure skater

SCOTT HAMILTON
figure skater

JEWEL
singer and poet

JAMES EARL JONES
actor

QUINCY JONES
musician and producer

ABRAHAM LINCOLN
U.S. president

WILLIAM PENN
Pennsylvania's founder

JACKIE ROBINSON
baseball legend

ROSEANNE
entertainer

MONICA SELES
tennis star

SAMMY SOSA
baseball star

DAVE THOMAS
entrepreneur

SHANIA TWAIN
entertainer

ROBIN WILLIAMS
performer

STEVIE WONDER
entertainer

ON FACING ADVERSITY

James Scott Brady

I GUESS IT'S a long way from a Centralia, Illinois, train yard to the George Washington University Hospital Trauma Unit. My dad was a yardmaster for the old Chicago, Burlington & Quincy Railroad. As a child, I used to get to sit in the engineer's lap and imagine what it was like to drive that train. I guess I always have liked being in the "driver's seat."

Years later, however, my interest turned from driving trains to driving campaigns. In 1979, former Texas governor John Connally hired me as a press secretary in his campaign for the American presidency. We lost the Republican primary to a former Hollywood star named Ronald Reagan. But I managed to jump over to the Reagan campaign. When Reagan was elected in 1980, I was "sitting in the catbird seat," as humorist James Thurber would say—poised to be named presidential press secretary. I held that title throughout the eight years of the Reagan administration. But not without one terrible, extended interruption.

It happened barely two months after the Reagan administration took office. I never even heard the shots. On March 30, 1981, my life went blank in an instant. In an attempt to assassinate President Reagan, John Hinckley Jr. armed himself with a "Saturday night special"—a low-quality, $29 pistol—and shot wildly as our presidential entourage exited a Washington hotel. One of the exploding bullets struck me just above the left eye. It shattered into a couple dozen fragments, some of which penetrated my skull and entered my brain.

INTRODUCTION

The next few months of my life were a nightmare of repeated surgery, broken contact with the outside world, and a variety of medical complications. More than once, I was very close to death.

The next few years were filled with frustrating struggles to function with a paralyzed right side, struggles to speak and communicate.

To people who face and defeat daunting obstacles, "ambition" is not becoming wealthy or famous or winning elections or awards. Words like "ambition" and "achievement" and "success" take on very different meanings. The objective is just to live, to wake up every morning. The goals are not lofty; they are very ordinary.

My own heroes are ordinary folks—but they accomplish extraordinary things because they try. My greatest hero is my wife, Sarah. She's accomplished a lot of things in life, but two stand out. The first has been the way she has cared for me and our son since I was shot. A tremendous tragedy and burden was dropped unexpectedly into her life, totally beyond her control and without justification. She could have given up; instead, she focused her energies on preserving our family and returning our lives to normal as much as possible. Week by week, month by month, year by year, she has not reached for the miraculous, just for the normal. Yet in focusing on the normal, she has helped accomplish the miraculous.

Her other most remarkable accomplishment, to me, has been spearheading the effort to keep guns out of the hands of criminals and children in America. Opponents call her a "gun grabber"; I call her a national hero. And I am not alone.

After a seven-year battle, during which Sarah and I worked tirelessly to educate the public about the need for stronger gun laws, the Brady Bill became law in 1993. It was a victory, achieved in the face of tremendous opposition, that now benefits all Americans. From the time the law took effect through fall 1997, background checks had stopped 173,000 criminals and other high-risk purchasers from buying handguns, and the law has helped to reduce illegal gun trafficking.

Sarah was not pursuing fame, or even recognition. She simply started at one point—when our son, Scott, found a loaded handgun on the seat of a pickup truck and, thinking it was a toy, pointed it at Sarah.

INTRODUCTION

Fortunately, no one was hurt. But seeing a gun nearly bring a second tragedy upon our family, Sarah became determined to do whatever she could to prevent senseless death and injury from guns.

Some people think of Sarah as a powerful political force. To me, she's the person who so many times fed me and helped me dress during my long years of recovery.

Overcoming obstacles is part of life, not just for people who are challenged by disabilities, illnesses, or tragedies, but for all people. No matter what the obstacle—fear, disability, prejudice, grief, or a difficulty that isn't likely to "just go away"—we can all work to make this world a better place.

With a powerful swing, Sammy Sosa connects off Milwaukee's Jason Bere for his 60th home run of the 1999 season.

1

THE 60–60 CLUB

THE CROWD IN CHICAGO'S Wrigley Field went crazy as Sammy Sosa walked to the plate to lead off the sixth inning. It was Saturday, September 18, 1999, and the Cubs had fallen behind the Milwaukee Brewers, 3-1. Time was running out for the home team, but if anyone could spark a comeback that afternoon, it was the tall, dark-skinned slugger who stood at the plate glaring at Brewers starting pitcher Jason Bere.

The Milwaukee hurler tried to be cautious. Sosa was one of the most dangerous hitters in the league. In 1998 he had engaged in a great competition for the major-league lead in home runs with Mark McGwire of the St. Louis Cardinals; together they had shattered a 37-year-old standard that had been set by Roger Maris in 1961. Sosa had finished second to McGwire with 66 home runs; in the 1999 season, he was trying to become the first player ever to hit 60 home runs in a season two times. His total for the year stood at 59. This led McGwire by three homers and was far better than everyone else in the major leagues.

Sammy had been in something of a rut in the preceeding games,

Is it going out? . . . Yes! Sammy watches the flight of number 60 from home plate, then waves to the crowd in excitement as he rounds the bases. On September 18, 1999, he became the first player in baseball history to hit 60 home runs twice in his career.

however. His last home run had come seven games earlier, on September 9 against the Cincinnati Reds.

Bere worked the count to 2-and-2, then threw a hard pitch toward the plate. It never reached the catcher. Sosa made contact and drove it deep toward center field. Brewers center fielder Marquis Grissom started running back to try and make a play but then stopped and watched the ball carry over the ivy-covered brick outfield wall.

As Sosa rounded the bases, everyone in the stadium stood and applauded. It was a great accomplishment for

the slugger, whose charm and grace during the intense pressure of the 1998 home-run race had made him one of the most popular professional athletes in the world.

Sammy's home run did seem to spark the Cubs. They scored again to tie the game at 3-all in the seventh inning. Then after Milwaukee went ahead 4-3 in the top of the ninth, Sammy Sosa was in the middle of another Cubs comeback. After Mark Grace led off the inning with a walk, Sammy singled him to third base. Grace eventually scored the tying run; Sammy, representing the winning run, reached third. Unfortunately the Cubs could not bring him home, and the game went into extra innings, with Milwaukee pulling out a 7-4 win in the 14th.

It was a moment typical of 1999 for Sammy Sosa: excitement at a personal accomplishment, accompanied by disappointment at his team's failure to win. The Cubs had won 90 games and reached the playoffs in 1998; Chicago was on its way to just a 67–95 record in 1999.

But despite the loss, Sammy was pleased and excited to become the charter member of the "60–60 club"—the first player ever to hit 60 home runs in back-to-back seasons. "I have to say that what I've done today is actually more special than what happened last year," Sosa commented afterward. "Mark [McGwire] did everything first last year. He was the man. This year the record is mine. It's something no one else has ever done. I'm extremely proud of that.

"I just felt good it happened here in Chicago in front of these great fans," he added. "I'm really happy to get it out of the way. I was really starting to press over the last couple of days."

Sosa's manager, Jim Riggleman, had high praise for his young star. "I am still amazed at Sammy Sosa, watching him day in and day out," Riggleman said. "Here's a guy that finds time to do everything, talk to the opposing players and manager, talk to the media and still outperform everyone in the game. It's been a great experience to be around Sammy Sosa." And even the opposing manager, Milwaukee's Jim Lefebvre, had something good to say. "I'm happy for him," Lefebvre, who had managed Sosa from 1992 to 1994, told reporters. "He's a class act and one of the real treasures we have in the game today. I'm glad he did it and he can say he has done what no one else has done."

Although by the end of the 1999 season Sosa would again wind up second to McGwire in the home-run race (McGwire finished with 65 to Sammy's 63), that did not diminish his stature in the eyes of his fans. Sammy's positive attitude during his pursuit of the home-run record had captured the hearts of millions of baseball fans. And thanks to his on-the-field exploits, his off-the-field good works, and his bubbly personality, "Slammin' Sammy" seemed destined to remain a favorite with the public.

"He had an absolutely wonderful year," McGwire said of Sammy as the 1999 season came to a close. "It's not the easiest thing to do coming to the ballpark every day when your team is in the position they're in. There's only two people in the world who know how difficult it is, him and me."

But Sammy Sosa has always insisted to sportswriters that he is just happy to be in the major leagues and able to perform consistently at a high level. "I enjoy everything I do," he says. "I'm happy." And the slugger, who grew up in poverty in the Dominican Republic, claims that the high expectations that come along with being one of the best players in the game today do not affect him at all. He has already had to overcome more than most people in order to make his dreams come true. "I never feel pressure," he told the media in 1998. "Pressure was when I was a kid and didn't have any food on the table."

The Dominican Republic, where Sammy Sosa grew up, is one of the poorest countries in the world. Sammy and his family struggled to survive, especially after the death of his father when Sammy was seven.

2
HUMBLE BEGINNINGS

THE MAN WE KNOW today simply as "Sammy" was born Samuel Peralta Sosa on November 12, 1968, in the Dominican Republic. He was the fifth of seven children born to Lucretia and Bautista Montero Sosa. When Sammy arrived, the family lived in Consuelo, a rural town a few miles outside San Pedro de Macorís.

The Dominican Republic shares the sunny island of Hispaniola with Haiti. Hispaniola lies southeast of Florida in the blue of the Caribbean Sea, with Puerto Rico on its eastern flank. The Dominican Republic takes up two-thirds of Hispaniola; the separate country of Haiti occupies the western third. A small country, the Dominican Republic measures just 235 miles across and 165 miles from north to south. The population is relatively small, about 8 million people. Many of them scratch out a living in the sugarcane fields.

Sammy's father, Bautista Montero Sosa, drove a tractor on a sugarcane plantation. His wages never provided more than the bare necessities. His family of nine lived in a two-room apartment in the back of what had formerly been a hospital. There were not enough beds for

Youngsters play baseball in the Dominican Republic, a small country located on an island in the Caribbean Sea. Baseball is the most popular sport in the Dominican Republic, and many great major-league players have come from the island.

everyone, so little Sammy had to sleep on the floor. On very warm nights, he slept outside. A sheet was all the covering he might need.

Although the Sosa family was poor, it was very close-knit and happy. There wasn't much room inside their home, so Sammy and his friends played outside a lot. Often they lacked shoes, so they ran along the local streets barefoot. Eventually, the family moved into San Pedro de Macorís. A seaport on the southeastern coast with over 125,000 residents, San Pedro de Macorís is the fourth-largest city in the Dominican Republic.

Tragedy struck when Sammy was seven years old: his 42-year-old father died. The family had been poor before; without Bautista's income they could barely survive. Everyone, even Sammy, had to find work. His mother started cooking lunches for workers in a local factory, while Sammy and his brother and sisters did whatever they could to earn money: washing cars, selling fruit on the street.

Soon Sammy and his brother José started shining shoes. They carried shoeshine boxes up and down the streets and along the beach looking for customers. A favorite spot was a tree-lined park in the center of town called the Parque Duarte. A shine earned them about 20 cents. They had to work all day to make $2.

Eventually Sammy's mother Lucretia remarried, but the family remained desperately poor. Years later, Sammy would remember wanting so badly to buy his mother a gift for Mother's Day that he begged for change until he had enough to buy her a cigarette.

Because he was often working, Sammy did not spend much time in school. But whenever he could steal some free time, he played sports with his friends. His first love was boxing, but he also enjoyed baseball. This is not surprising; baseball is the most popular sport in the Dominican Republic. There is a six-month period when the sugarcane fields do not need attention, so many unemployed workers turn to baseball to pass the time. San Pedro de Macorís has been called the Baseball Capital of the World; a greater percentage of players from San Pedro reach the major leagues than from any other town in the world. "[Baseball is] more than a game," a Dominican baseball manager named Winston Llenas once said. "It's our passion. It's our way of life."

The kids in Sammy's neighborhood were too poor to afford real baseball equipment, so they made their own. For a glove, they would cut two pieces of cardboard into the shape of a glove, then fill in the middle with pieces of discarded burlap bags for cushioning. They would then sew up the sides with fishing line and beat a pocket in the middle with their fists. Sammy's first glove was made from an inside-out milk carton. The vasima trees that

Roberto Clemente, a great star for the Pittsburgh Pirates, was one of Sammy's heroes when he was growing up. Clemente, an 11-time All-Star, recorded 3,000 hits and a .317 batting average in his 18-year career with the Pirates.

grew in the neighborhood provided branches that could be carved into rough bats. And since the poor neighborhood kids could not afford a real baseball, Sammy's first games were played using a homemade ball. The neighborhood kids would find an old golf ball, wrap it with torn nylon stockings that their mothers were throwing away, then take this makeshift baseball to a local shoemaker. For 50 cents he would sew a leather cover around the ball. If they did not have the 50 cents, they simply wrapped the stocking-covered golf ball with black tape.

As Sammy learned about baseball, he also learned about some of the great players who had left the Dominican Republic and the other countries of Latin America to play in the major leagues in the United States. One of the most famous was a Puerto Rican outfielder named Roberto Clemente, who compiled 3,000 hits, four batting titles, and a .317 batting average during his Hall-of-Fame career. Clemente is often regarded as the finest player to come from Latin America, and he is also seen as a great humanitarian because of the money and time that he donated back to that area. The 38-year-old Clemente was flying with a relief mission bringing medical and food supplies to earthquake-torn Nicaragua on New Year's Eve 1972 when his airplane crashed into the ocean. Among the great Dominican players of the 1960s and 1970s were hard-throwing pitcher Juan Marichal, who won 243 games and struck out more than 2,300 batters, and brothers Felipe, Matty, and Jesus Alou.

Sammy loved to compete on the baseball field, but he also competed in life. The difference between eating and going hungry might depend on whether Sammy won a race with 20 other shoeshine boys to reach a tourist first and ask if he wanted his shoes polished.

One day in 1979, Sammy was the first shoeshine boy to reach a man named Bill Chase. The 11-year-old could not know at the time that Chase would turn out to be a friend and benefactor. Chase was a U.S. citizen who was opening a shoe factory in San Pedro de Macorís.

"There was this little kid with this big smile," Chase later recalled. "I said to him, 'Do you want to shine my shoes?' He said yes. It was Sammy."

Bill Chase was impressed by the boy's big smile and enthusiasm. Bill would get many more shines from the Sosa brothers, and eventually he invited them to help around the factory. Sammy and Juan carried messages, ran errands, and shined shoes.

With the extra money coming in from their work in the factory, Sammy did not have to work all the time. He could spend more of his time playing baseball. Sammy liked to play at a field in the neighborhood known as the Barrio Mexico. There he met Hector Sterling, a former player for the University of Santo Domingo's baseball team who taught the neighborhood kids the fundamentals of the game. Hector became Sammy's first coach. At first, Hector played Sammy at second base, but he soon moved him to the outfield to take advantage of his speedy long legs.

One day Bill Chase returned from a trip to the United States with a real leather baseball glove. It was a present for Sammy. The gift both surprised and inspired the teenager. Sammy began practicing harder. In the next couple of years, others in San Pedro began to recognize the talents of this tall, thin outfielder with a wild but powerful swing.

The professional baseball draft does not extend to the

Dominican Republic, so major-league teams send scouts there to find talent. The kids of San Pedro de Macorís had such superb natural baseball talent that big-league scouts visited Hector's baseball school, as well as the other baseball diamonds of San Pedro, on a regular basis. The visiting scouts noticed Sammy early.

When Sammy was 15—only a year after he began to play the game under Hector's guidance—the Philadelphia Phillies offered him a contract to play in the States on one of their farm teams. He signed it immediately. Looking back, he would reminisce, "I did not care who I signed with. I only cared about signing and playing." He loved the game but also clearly understood that a baseball career could well be a ticket to provide for his family—that if he succeeded, he would be able to help them escape their life in poverty. But baseball officials in the United States ordered the Phillies to cancel the contract. Sammy was too young, they said. For the moment, his hopes were dashed.

A year later, however, Sammy would get another chance. During a short trip around the Dominican Republic, Amado Dinzey, a scout for the Texas Rangers, had seen Sammy play. He told another Rangers scout, Omar Minaya, about the young outfielder from San Pedro. Minaya flew to the Dominican Republic and got in touch with Sammy. He told him the complimentary things Amado had said and asked Sammy to come to a tryout camp.

Sammy was delighted. The 16-year-old borrowed an old uniform and a pair of cleats that had holes in the soles from a friend, and rode the bus for four hours to the tryout. Sammy was not physically imposing—standing about 5 feet 10 inches tall and weighing about 150 pounds—but he was quick, running 60 yards in 7.5 seconds.

"He almost looked as if he was malnourished," Omar Minaya later said. "I noticed some of the balls he hit to the outfield. They'd run out of steam, and to me that was malnourishment. But I noticed something else even more, Sammy's bat speed. And there was another thing. I sensed something inside him, a kind of fire. Right from the start you could see how aggressive he was."

Minaya decided that Sammy might one day develop into a first-rate ballplayer. The scout offered him a professional contract with the Texas Rangers, with a $3,000 bonus.

Sammy was being offered the chance to pursue his dream of professional baseball. Nevertheless, Sammy didn't immediately accept Minaya's offer. He made a counteroffer, asking for $4,000. Minaya must have smiled; Sammy was showing he was going to be aggressive off as well as on the field. They finally settled on $3,500.

Sammy gave nearly every penny he received up front to his mother, although he did use a little to buy his first bicycle. But he didn't have much time to ride it, for he soon had to leave the Dominican Republic for Florida to start his professional baseball career.

Sammy Sosa (at right) in a Texas Rangers uniform during 1988 spring training. The Rangers had signed Sammy to his first big-league contract two years earlier. With him are minor-league teammates Tony Scruggs (left) and Juan Gonzalez, who would go on to win the American League's MVP Award in 1996 and 1998.

3

A TEEN IN THE MINOR LEAGUES

SAMMY'S FAMILY ACCOMPANIED him to the airport for the flight to the United States. Sammy's mom was crying as he turned to walk to the plane. She was worried about her 17-year-old son. How could he survive in a foreign country? He could speak only a few words of English. America was a land of tremendous opportunity, but it was also a land of temptations and dangers for a poor teenager alone away from home.

Walking toward the plane, Sammy's heart must have raced with excitement. While he loves his country and returns there as often as possible, he would explain later, "My dream was to get to the United States any way I could. I never could think about things like records or what I might do in baseball. I never had time for that. I only wanted to get to this beautiful country."

When Sammy Sosa arrived in the United States in 1986, he had already carried adult burdens for 10 years, helping to support his family any way he could. Now he faced new challenges: the problem of racism and the danger of drugs. Sammy managed to avoid these problems, but he still found his move to the United States hard. He missed his close-knit family and suffered from homesickness. Sammy sent most of every paycheck home to his mother. He even shared an apartment with five other players, so he could send back more money. "For the Dominican, our family comes first," he later said. "[Dominican players] are always going . . . to take care of 'my mother, my father, my cousin, my aunt'—everybody."

One big problem he faced was that he spoke very little English. Fortunately, he made friends with some other Latin American players. Sammy would go out with them to eat. He couldn't read the menus, so he just ordered whatever they did. It was difficult for him to be out by himself—to ask directions, for example. His lack of English also occasionally made things hard for him on the baseball diamond. But he quickly learned enough English to get by. He soon could order food, get wherever he wanted to go, and most importantly, understand his teammates and coaches.

"It wasn't easy then," Sammy remembered. "At the beginning, it was a little hard for me because my English was not the way it is now. I got lucky because there were some Puerto Rican players whom I hung out with. They helped me out a lot. This is the way I was able to understand the life here in the United States. After I had the opportunity to get past that transition, everything became easier."

Everyone who saw Sammy when he started playing with a Rangers farm team in Florida agreed that he had raw talent and decent prospects. However, he had a lot to learn, and was going to have to work and work and work if he wanted to be one of the handful of players that actually reach the majors.

Every year the big-league teams sign hundreds of young men who show some baseball talent. Then they send them to affiliated minor-league teams, where they receive experience and expert coaching. In the minors, players find out whether they can play the kind of pro ball that can take them to the majors. Many can't—only one in 14 minor-league players ever makes it to the majors.

There are four levels of minor-league baseball: rookie ball, Class A, Class AA, and Class AAA. Each time a player moves to a new level, he finds it harder to excel. Mistakes or flaws in a player's game, like difficulty hitting a curve or control problems when pitching, are magnified as the quality of the competition improves.

Felipe Alou, a native of the Dominican Republic who starred in the major leagues from 1958 to 1972, then became a coach and manager with the Montreal Expos, talked about how scouts sign any player who exhibits talent in hopes that he will develop, even though the player may not have all the tools necessary for big-league success. "They sign 25 guys and maybe only one is a good player," Alou said. "It's like they throw a net in the ocean, hoping that maybe they'll get a big fish. The problem is, if they don't get a big fish, they'll throw all the smaller ones back."

Sammy started his professional baseball career in 1986 in Sarasota, Florida, with the Rangers' rookie-league team in the Gulf Coast League. He played all 61 games on the team's schedule, and rapped out 63 hits in 229 at bats for a .275 batting average. He slammed four homers, drove in 28 runs, and showed his speed by hitting a league-leading 19 doubles and stealing 11 bases.

At the end of the season, Sammy flew home. Some minor-league players spend their off-seasons resting and relaxing. After all, life in the minor leagues can be draining because of the enormous amount of time teams spend traveling to games played away from the home field. But other players, like Sammy, never put down their bats for long. Sammy played for a pro club in the Dominican Republic over the winter.

In the spring of 1987, the start of a new season in the States, Sammy reported to the Rangers' Class-A team in Gastonia, North Carolina.

Playing the outfield every day, Sammy continued to improve. Yet he still had a lot to learn about basic defensive skills. Most professional players start learning the game when they are six or seven years old. By the time they sign a contract, they may have played and been coached for a dozen years. Although 18-year-old Sammy was in his second year of pro ball, he had just started playing baseball under the eye of a coach four years earlier. He was still assimilating the fundamentals of the game—which base to throw the ball to in different situations or whether to throw ahead of or behind the runner. These are all split-second decisions players have to make during the heat of the action. Games can be lost because of one bad throw or defensive lapse, and a player who does not know what to do in every defensive situation will have trouble moving up in organized baseball.

The best way to learn is through experience. As Sammy learned, he made his share of costly errors. But his coaches were patient with Sammy because he always worked hard to improve and learn from his mistakes.

In the United States, Sammy was eating better than he ever had at home, and the Rangers also provided nutritional supplements to combat the effects of his malnourished childhood. Sammy's frame began filling out to an even 6 feet tall and 185 pounds.

His bat speed and powerful swing kept managers interested in Sammy. He had the prospects of a slugger. Bat speed is what drives the ball—the faster the better. By the end of his second season in the minors, Sammy showed some improvement at the plate. His batting average had risen slightly, from .275 to .279, and he had racked up 59 RBIs, with 27 doubles, 4 triples, and 11 homers. He had also stolen 22 bases and scored more runs, 73, than anyone else on his team.

However, in the field Sammy made 17 defensive errors, a very high number for an outfielder, and at the plate he struck out 123 times in 129 games. "He swung at every ball, I think," said Mike Scott, the Rangers' former director of player development. "But the tools were always there—the above-average power, arm, speed. It was just a matter of adjusting to curves in the dirt, hitting to right on outside pitches. I think his most important number was at-bats. He didn't experience great success, and it made him work harder."

Even though the Gastonia team boasted several future major-league superstars in addition to Sammy—including two-time American League Most Valuable Player Juan Gonzalez, a native of Puerto Rico who had been signed at the same time as Sammy, and hard-throwing pitcher Kevin Brown—it was not a very good season. Gastonia ended 1987 with a 58–82 record, finishing 11th among the 12 teams in the South Atlantic League.

The next year, 1988, Sammy moved to another Single-A team affiliated with the Rangers, Port Charlotte of the Florida State League. He played hard, perhaps inspired by a story that appeared in a Dominican newspaper in April reporting that the 35 Dominicans then playing in the major leagues were earning a combined salary of nearly $15.5 million. Unfortunately, Sammy may have pressed a little *too* hard in his quest to join his countrymen in the major leagues immediately. He stole 42 bases and scored 70 runs at Port Charlotte, but his batting average dropped off dramatically to just .229, and he managed just 9 home runs and 51 RBIs in 507 at-bats.

Omar Minaya, the scout who had signed Sammy, felt he understood why Sammy was swinging at pitches that were balls when he should have been waiting patiently for strikes within his preferred batting zone. "You've got to understand something about Latin players when they are young—or really any players from low economic backgrounds," he explained. "They know the only way to make money is by putting up offensive numbers." Sammy himself would eventually agree with this assessment. "It's not easy for a Latin player to take 100 walks," he once commented. "If I knew the stuff I know now 7 years ago—taking pitches, being more relaxed—I would have put up even better numbers. But people have to understand where you're coming from."

In the off-season, Sammy again returned to the Dominican Republic. There he played with the team in Santo Domingo, the country's capital. This was an opportunity to continue working on the skills he had been learning from the Rangers' coaches. When the team won the Caribbean World Series, Sammy and the other players each received 1,200 pesos (about $300). He gave the money to his mother.

Even though he had put up poor stats at Port Charlotte in 1988, Sammy was moved up to the next minor-league level the following year. He was now 20 years old, and the Rangers needed to know whether he would be able to compete. At the start of the 1989 season, Sammy reported to the Tulsa Drillers of the Class AA Texas League.

By now Sammy was getting used to life in the United States, thanks largely to his improved English-language skills. Few Dominicans live in Tulsa, but he managed to get along. He stayed in close touch with his family and returned to the Dominican Republic often. By now he'd become, in effect, a resident of two countries, both of which he loved. This in itself was a major adjustment for a young man of 20.

In the first 66 games of the 1989 season, Sammy batted .297, his best average yet in the minors. He also hit 7 home runs and drove in 31 baserunners. His hitting and speed impressed the Texas Rangers. In June, Sammy got the call he'd been waiting for—the Rangers were bringing him up to join the big-league team.

On June 16, 1989, 20-year-old Sammy appeared in his first major-league game, against the New York Yankees. He quickly recorded his first hit, off Yankees starter Andy Hawkins, and finished the day 2-for-4. Five days later, on June 21, Sammy belted his first major-league home run in

In his first few years in professional baseball, first with the Rangers' organization and later with the Chicago White Sox, Sammy had to work as hard on his fielding as on his hitting. In the minors, Sammy often had long talks with teammate Juan Gonzalez on what they had to do to succeed. "We realized we had to go out there every day, work on our hitting, and take fly balls every day," he later said.

a game against the Boston Red Sox. The homer was even more impressive because the pitcher who served it up to Sammy was one of the best in the American League: Roger Clemens, a hard-throwing righthander who had won the Cy Young Award, baseball's highest pitching award, in 1986 and 1987.

Sammy stayed with the Rangers for about a month and played nearly every day in the outfield. However, he struggled with major-league pitching and hit just .238. He

Roger Clemens, one of the best pitchers in baseball in the 1980s and 1990s, perhaps took Rangers rookie Sammy Sosa too lightly. The first time Sosa faced "the Rocket," on August 21, 1989, Sammy took him deep for his first major-league home run.

exhibited little power—16 of his 20 hits were singles—and was thrown out both times he tried to steal a base. He also was still making mistakes in the outfield. The Rangers were in the middle of a pennant race, and they needed an outfielder who could both hit and field well. Sammy did not seem to be ready yet.

On July 20, after 25 games, Sammy was sent back down to the minors. This time, though, Sammy was sent to the Rangers' top farm team, the Class AAA Oklahoma City 89ers.

Sammy must have taken his demotion hard. He played in 10 games for the 89ers but managed just four hits in 39 plate appearances—a miniscule .103 batting average.

Then, on July 29, he was part of a trade between Texas and the Chicago White Sox. The Rangers sent Sammy and another minor-league prospect, pitcher Wilson Alvarez, as well as infielder Scott Fletcher, to the Chicago White Sox. In exchange the Rangers received outfielder Harold Baines, a good hitter who had made the All-Star team with the Sox that year, and infielder Fred Manrique.

The White Sox immediately assigned Sammy to their Triple-A farm team in Vancouver. But Sammy played only 13 games for the Vancouver Canadians. In those 13 games, Sammy's batting average soared to .367. Thanks to his performance in Vancouver, Sammy was called back up to the major leagues late in 1989. This time he'd be wearing a White Sox uniform.

Sammy in his White Sox uniform. After being traded by the Rangers, he played well with the Sox in 1989, batting .273 in 33 games.

4
MAKING IT IN THE MAJORS

ON AUGUST 22, 1989, Sammy played his first game for the Chicago White Sox. He gave the fans a taste of things to come in the game against the Minnesota Twins, going 3-for-3 with a home run and two RBIs. This was a good start, and Sammy continued to play well for the White Sox. He appeared in 33 games with the team in 1989, batting .273 with five doubles, three homers, ten RBIs, and seven stolen bases.

Some very good baseball players spend their entire careers in the minor leagues. It had taken Sammy Sosa less than four years to become a regular in the major leagues. Now he would have to work hard to stay there. "I need to work hard every day on everything," he admitted to reporters. "In baseball, you need to work hard every day, day by day."

In the next season, 1990, thanks to hard work Sammy held onto his starting spot in the outfield. His game still needed improvement. Sammy batted just .233 and struck out 150 times. But on the positive side, he hit 15 homers, drove in 70 runs, and was the only player in the major leagues to reach double figures in doubles (26), triples (10), home runs, and stolen bases (32). He was also getting better as a defensive player. Although he made 13 errors, still a high figure for an outfielder, Sammy also threw out 14 baserunners, ranking him second in the league.

Some people complained that Sammy was not a "team player"—that he was more interested in his own statistics than in helping his team win. Perhaps this was linked to his desire to help his family and friends financially. Historian Robert Klein, writing generally on players from the Dominican Republic, has noted, "Poverty increases the pressure to succeed in the major leagues. Not only does a player's family depend on his success but often his entire community does as well, and since Dominican ballplayers have been so talented, the expectations are high." And as Jaime Torres, an agent for Latino players in the United States, points out, "There's always that status. . . . But unfortunately in the Dominican Republic when a player gets released, you wouldn't believe the shame. You're worthless. This is a failure. He was given the opportunity and he failed."

Sammy himself admitted that he would rather try to hit a home run than work a pitcher for a walk, but argued that his motivations actually were team oriented. "[T]hey said I was a selfish player because I wanted to do everything for myself," he later said. "That's not right. When you pay somebody, you want that guy to do everything for you, right? So you're not going to pay a guy, when you have a man on second and a man on third, to take a walk. You know what I mean? When the pressure's on, I'm the man. I want to be there."

After the 1990 season, Sammy was making enough money that he could afford to build a house for his mother. He had it equipped with two possessions that Americans generally take for granted—a television and a telephone. These were both firsts for the Sosa family in the Dominican Republic.

Ozzie Guillen, a veteran White Sox infielder, once

asked Sammy, "Why do you think about money so much?" "I've got to take care of my family," Sosa replied. Guillen advised the younger player, "Don't think about money. Just go out and play, and the money will be there. It will take a while."

Despite his hard work, Sammy was faced with the prospect of failure in 1991. Although he started off the season by hitting two homers and driving in five runs in the opening game, his production tailed off after that. He was taken out of the starting lineup on April 22. Even though he was working every day with Walt Hriniak, the hitting coach for the White Sox, his batting average had fallen under .200. On July 19, the Sox sent him back to the minor leagues, to their Triple-A club in Vancouver, Canada.

In the 32 games that Sammy played for the Canadians, he seemed to get his batting stroke back. He hit .267 with 3 home runs and 19 RBIs. On August 27, the White Sox brought Sammy back up. Even though Sammy continued to struggle against big-league pitching, he played the rest of the season with the Sox.

When the season ended, Sammy had just a .203 batting average and 10 home runs in 116 games with Chicago. Although he had some good moments, he was still trying too hard to hit home runs. On the whole, it had been a miserable baseball year for Sammy Sosa.

But things started looking up after the season ended. In November he married the woman he had been dating for several years, Sonia Esther. They had met in a dance club in Santo Domingo when she was 17 years old and working on a variety show that aired on Dominican television.

Sammy kisses his wife, Sonia, during Sammy Sosa Day festivities at Wrigley Field in 1998. The couple met as Sammy was trying to make it in the big leagues, and were married in November 1991.

Making contact: Sosa showed slugging potential in 1990, when he hit 15 home runs for the Sox, but he struggled at the plate the next season, batting just .203.

Sammy, who was home for the off-season, saw her across the room and was smitten. He asked a waiter to carry her a note: "If you will do me the honor of having one dance with me, it will be the start of a beautiful friendship."

"I like guys who are big, tall and dark," Sonia later recalled. "I looked at him and said, 'Oh wow—what a man.'" She had no idea he was a professional baseball player on the way up to fame and fortune or that becoming involved with him would take her to the United States.

Although after his marriage his personal life was more settled—Sammy was devoted to his wife, and in the next four years they would have four children—his baseball career was floundering. Fans continued to see him as a player too interested in his own stats, at the expense of winning. He did not try to advance runners with sacrifice hits or walks, and he took too many risks stealing bases.

However, some baseball insiders recognized that, at age 21, Sammy was just trying too hard. He still had a long way to go before he could catch up, in terms of experience, with American players who had gotten an earlier start in organized baseball.

One person who believed in Sammy's potential was Larry Himes. In 1989 Himes had been the general manager of the White Sox, and had put together the trade that brought Sosa over from the Rangers. After the 1992 season, he left the Sox and moved across town to take a job with the Chicago Cubs. He still believed in Sammy's potential and thought that White Sox batting coach Walt Hriniak had tried too hard to change Sammy's style, negatively affecting his batting stats.

On March 30, 1992, Sammy and Sonia learned that Himes had traded for the young slugger once again. He sent George Bell, a home-run hitter from the Dominican Republic, to the White Sox; in exchange, the Cubs received Sosa and relief pitcher Ken Patterson. (Interestingly, at one time when Sammy was growing up, he had washed Bell's car to earn extra cash)

Sammy liked Chicago, and he was glad that he was just moving to a different team in the same city. The Cubs were one of the oldest baseball franchises. When the team had been started in the 1870s, it had been called the White Stockings, but by the start of the 20th century it was known as the Cubs.

Cubs fans have the dubious distinction of suffering through more losing years than the fans of any other team in major-league baseball. In 1906 the Cubs lost the World

Series to their crosstown rivals, the White Sox, then rebounded to win the championship in 1907 and 1908. The Cubs would not reach the World Series again until 1945, when they lost in seven games to the Detroit Tigers, and the team has not been back since. Even playoff appearances are rare: the Cubs won the National League East division in 1984 and 1989, but lost in the League Championship Series each year.

Fans of the Chicago Cubs learned long ago that it is possible to enjoy a baseball game even if your team doesn't win. They follow their team enthusiastically, attending the games in historic Wrigley Field, with its ivy-covered brick outfield walls.

Although Chicago had won the division title just three years before Sammy joined the team, it had gone into a decline immediately afterward. In 1991 the Cubs had finished with a losing record, 77–85. To improve, they needed a power hitter. Manager Jim Lefebvre promised Sammy that as long as he worked hard, he would play every day, even if he did make mistakes. Sammy would start in center field, rather than in right, because a superstar named Andre Dawson was holding down the right-field job in Chicago. This meant Sammy would have to concentrate on his defense as well as his hitting, because center field is the most difficult outfield position to play.

Earlier in his career, Sammy had worn uniform number 25. But the Cubs assigned him number 21—the same number that Roberto Clemente, one of his boyhood heroes, had worn for the Pirates during his Hall-of-Fame career. Perhaps that would be a good omen.

From the start of the 1992 season, Sammy Sosa took the antics of the Cubs' fans in good humor. He talked and joked with the crowd. In return, he became a fan favorite.

Sammy didn't play very well in the first 24 games of the season, hitting just .211. But as promised, Cubs management left him in the lineup. All hitters go through slumps. On May 7, Sammy hit his first homer as a Cub.

On June 10, he hit the long ball twice in a single game. But just three nights later, on June 13, Sammy was hit by an inside fastball that broke a bone in his hand. He was not able to play, and the Cubs placed him on the disabled list (DL) until July 27.

When Sammy finally got back in the lineup, he hit a home run in his first at-bat. Over the next nine games, Sammy batted .385 with 3 home runs and 9 RBIs. But on August 7, he fouled a pitch that hit his left ankle so hard that the bone fractured. Sammy was placed on the disabled list again. Disappointingly, he would miss the rest of the season.

Sammy finished with a .260 batting average, his highest in the majors to date. In 67 games, he scored 41 runs, slugged 8 homers, and drove in 25 baserunners.

The Cubs, who ended the year 78–84, remained committed to Sammy. After all, not many players could compete in the major leagues at his age. But it was clear that he still had a lot to learn.

"When he first got here you could see he had great physical skills, but he was so raw. He didn't know how to play the game," remembered veteran Cubs teammate Mark Grace. "He didn't understand the concept of hitting behind runners. He didn't understand the concept of hitting the cutoff man to keep a double play in order. So many little things he just didn't know."

In the off-season, Sammy and Sonia returned to the Dominican Republic, where Sammy played winter ball. Every day, he worked out in the weight room, trying to get stronger, and he also fine-tuned his timing in the batter's box. Andre Dawson had left the Cubs to sign with Boston as a free agent, so Sammy anticipated that the right-field job would be his and hoped that his hard work would pay off in 1993.

Sammy Sosa struggled at the plate in the major leagues until 1992, when he began working with Cubs batting coach Billy Williams. The results were immediate: in 1993 Sammy hit more home runs, drove in more runs, and had a higher batting average than he had ever had in a full season. Here, Sosa and Williams share a laugh in the dugout.

5

BECOMING A STAR

WHEN SAMMY SOSA began playing with the Cubs, he was a dead pull hitter. This means that, because he batted from the right side, he rarely got a hit to right field. His power stroke always drove the ball to left field. This is common with many sluggers.

Sammy knew that by learning to hit to the opposite field, he would be a better hitter. He wanted to learn how to dump an outside pitch into right field. Billy Williams, the Cubs' batting coach, wanted to help. Williams had put together a Hall-of-Fame career as a player with the Cubs during the 1960s and early 1970s, pounding out 2,711 hits, 426 home runs, and a career batting average of .290. He recognized that Sammy needed a lot of coaching to grow and reach his full potential.

Slowly and patiently, Williams taught Sammy to stop lunging out over the plate with his body to hit a curve ball that was tailing away from him. He coached Sammy to let unhittable pitches go by, to stand farther back in the batter's box, and not to open his shoulder too soon when he was swinging. These are basic hitting principles, but Sammy had never had a coach take enough time to go over them with him

One of the highlights of Sammy's great 1993 season was joining the "30–30 club"—a nickname given to the handful of players who have stolen 30 or more bases and hit 30 or more home runs in a single season.

before. He immediately began to improve at the plate.

With new confidence in his hitting, Sammy started the 1993 season strong, and he just kept improving. On May 4, he banged out five hits—including two homers—in six at-bats. When he picked up three hits in his final three times at the plate on May 30, then went 6-for-6 in the next game, his nine consecutive hits broke a team record. In one stretch of games between June 28 and July 4, Sammy batted .538, with 14 hits in 26 at-bats, and was named

National League Player of the Week for the first time. By September 2, he had already jacked 30 homers for the year, and on September 29, Cubs fans went wild when he stole four bases in a single game. Sammy was the first Chicago Cub ever to join the "30–30 club"—hitting 30 home runs and stealing 30 bases in the same season.

Sammy finished with a .261 average, 33 roundtrippers, 36 stolen bases, and 93 RBIs. Defensively, he played well and showed that baserunners ran on his powerful arm at their own peril. He recorded 17 assists, second best in the National League.

"That was the first season in which I really felt comfortable," Sammy later commented. And as he emerged as a star, the Cubs improved as well. Chicago ended the season with a winning record, and coaches, sportswriters, and fans gave Sammy a lot of the credit for the team's improvement.

By this time, Sammy was a millionaire. For years he had sent all his money home. Now, though, he was making enough to support his mother, brother, and sisters in the Dominican Republic *and* indulge his wife and children as well. He had already bought his mother a third new house in the Dominican Republic. For his own family he had purchased a luxury apartment on the 55th floor of a swanky building in downtown Chicago with a spectacular view of the city.

The boy who had once worked for nickels and dimes now spoiled himself as well. Sammy bought new cars and fancy clothes. He also had a huge gold necklace made that boasted the numbers "30–30" and was covered with jewels. He wore the heavy jewelry proudly, holding it up for the crowds in the hometown stands. This gave him something of a reputation as a showoff and a spendthrift.

Today Sammy laughs about the gaudy jewelry. He no longer wears the pendant, but keeps it at his home in the Dominican Republic along with other trophies and awards he has received. "Sometimes you do some things," he later commented. "And after a while you think, 'Wow, I shouldn't have done that.'" However, those fans who criticized Sammy for his jewelry probably did not realize how poor he had been growing up and how much it had meant to him to achieve stardom in the big leagues.

When the 1994 season began, morale in the clubhouse and fans' expectations were both higher than they had been for a long time. And Sammy Sosa picked up where he had left off in 1993. By August 11 he had belted 25 homers and driven in 70 runs in 105 games. He was leading the team in hitting, with a career-best .300 batting average, and had stolen a team-high 22 bases. In fact, he seemed to be getting better every day: in the team's previous 22 games, Sammy rapped out hits at a .358 clip.

Unfortunately, the 1994 season ended the next day, August 12, when the baseball players went on strike. The final third of the games were cancelled, and for the first time in more than 90 years, the World Series was not held.

The fall of 1994 was a sad time for baseball fans. The strike dragged on so long that the next season started late. In the meantime, many fans had become angry with the players and team owners, both of whom they considered greedy.

Sammy was as relieved as most ballplayers when the strike was finally settled. He had two families to support. He signed a one-year, $4 million contract with the Cubs for the 1995 season. This was the most money he had ever earned and would ensure financial security for his families. After years of worrying about money, he could finally relax and play ball.

The 1995 season was fun for the Cubs and their fans. Chicago had a new manager, Jim Riggleman, and Sammy's power hitting was an important part of the team's success. The Cubs were even competing for the top spot in the new National League Central division. (After the strike ended, the National and American leagues had been reorganized into three divisions; under the new rules each division winner would make the league playoffs, while the second-place team with the best record would also reach the postseason as a "wild card" entry.)

Sammy was hitting plenty of balls out of the park. In fact he was among the league leaders in home runs. At the end of June he was selected as an alternate for the 1995 All-Star Game. He played but went hitless in one at-bat.

On one glorious afternoon in July, Sammy reached a milestone with his 100th major-league home run. In August he went on a hitting tear, pounding 13 homers and driving in 32 runs in 20 games. One of these home runs, on August 14, was the 10,000th home run hit in the 120-year history of the Chicago franchise. Sammy's slugging kept the Cubs in the playoff race through August.

"Sammy can carry a club," recognized club president Andy McPhail. "The last few weeks, when we have asserted ourselves and played better in the bigger games, Sammy has had more to do with that than any other player."

Although Sammy continued hitting the ball hard and was even named Player of the Week at the start of September, the rest of the team cooled off down the stretch. The Cubs finished out of the playoff picture by four games, finishing third in the NL Central. But Chicago's 73–71 record was just the team's second winning season since 1989.

Sammy had played all 144 games of the shortened season. He batted .268 and set new career highs in homers with 36 (which tied him for second in the National League) and RBIs with 119 (the second-best total in the league). His 34 steals were the seventh-best figure in the league. At the end of the season, the *Sporting News* chose him for its National League All-Star Team.

The Cubs rewarded Sammy's fine play with a new two-year contract worth more than $10 million. Sammy had arrived.

After the deal was announced, Sammy talked about his desire to repay the team for its belief in him. "I want to be one of the best players in the game. Billy Williams, Roberto Clemente—that's the level I'm trying to get to," he said. "I have a good long career ahead of me." But when sportswriters compared him to the great Clemente, Sammy wisely responded, "I'd like to have his career, but I can only play like Sammy Sosa. People have to tell me if I play like him; I can't tell myself."

Sammy started the 1996 season well. He socked two home runs in the same inning in a game against the Houston Astros on May 16, a feat that only a few players have ever accomplished. On June 5 he hit three homers in the same game for the first time. By the All-Star break, Sammy was leading the league in home runs. However, he was not chosen for the National League All-Star team.

In July, Sammy made All-Star Team manager Bobby Cox regret his decision not to pick him for the squad. He maintained his league lead in homers and batted .358 for the month, leading to his selection as Player of the Month.

On August 20, still leading the league in homers, Sammy was hit in the right wrist by a pitch thrown by the Marlins' Mark Hutton. He required surgery to repair the resulting broken bone. The Cubs placed Sammy on the disabled list; he was out for the rest of the season.

This was a big disappointment, as Sammy had been headed for his best year ever. He had hit 40 home runs, four more than his previous best total, and driven in an even 100 runs while playing in just 124 games.

Sammy was frustrated watching the Cubs' games but not being able to play. Without him in the lineup, the Cubs slipped to 76–86. "I'd go there, watch the games, and do nothing," he said. "I hope that never happens to me again." But Sammy swallowed his frustration and used the enforced free time to think of new ways he could give something back to his native country.

In 1996 Sammy Sosa financed the construction of a $1.2 million shopping center in San Pedro de Macorís. He hoped this would stimulate the economy of his home town. The shopping center was named the 30-30 Plaza, commemorating Sammy's breakthrough 1993 season. It was located not far from the park where Sammy had once shined shoes, so he dedicated the mall to the shoeshine boys of the Dominican Republic. In the center of the plaza, a fountain with a statue of Sammy was built. All of the coins that are thrown into this fountain are used for the benefit of shoeshine boys. Inside the mall, Sammy opened businesses for his sisters and a nightclub called Club Sammy.

The 30–30 Plaza, a shopping center in San Pedro de Macorís that was financed by Sammy Sosa in 1996, boasts a statue of the Cubs' slugger in the center of a fountain dedicated to Dominican shoeshine boys.

Sammy has done many other nice things for the people of the Dominican Republic. He bought an ambulance for the fire department of San Pedro because it could not afford to purchase one. Over the years he would arrange for hundreds of computers to be donated to Dominican schools.

He also started his own baseball academy in San Pedro de Macorís, the Sammy Sosa *Escuela de Beisbol*. Sammy has spent over $300,000 on the school, which has playing fields and dormitories where students can stay. "Sammy's idea was to give these guys the facilities and teachers to learn the game of baseball that he did not have," explained Juan Francisco Tolentino, one of the school's permanent coaches.

And there were personal highlights in the off-season as well. In October, Sonia Sosa gave birth to the couple's third child. After two daughters, they had a baby boy who was named after his father: Sammy Jr.

The 1997 season was a great one for Sammy Sosa: he recorded the 1,000th base hit and 200th home run of his career in August.

6

LEARNING TO BE PATIENT

AFTER HIS INJURY-SHORTENED season of 1996, Sammy was determined to come back strongly in 1997. For the first time, he didn't play winter ball in the Dominican Republic. He wanted his hand to heal completely, so that he could concentrate on the new season ahead and report to spring training in top shape.

Both Sammy and the Cubs started out slowly. The team had been picked by some sportswriters to compete for the NL Central title, but playoff hopes all but went out the window when Chicago lost its first 14 games. Sammy hit poorly in the first month of the season.

In May, his bat finally started to warm up. On May 16 Sammy drove in a career-high six runs in a game, going 4-for-4 with a homer and a triple. During one six-game stretch in May, he smashed the ball at a .348 clip, with 4 homers, 2 triples, and 12 RBIs. On May 26th, Sammy hit an inside-the-park home run at Pittsburgh. Obviously, the injury that had cut his season short in 1996 was not slowing him down at all in 1997.

The Cubs recognized the importance of a healthy Sammy Sosa to their club. In June they signed him to a new four-year contract worth $42.5 million. The deal made Sammy the third-highest paid player in the major leagues, behind only superstars Barry Bonds and Albert Belle. Team management made it clear that the contract was both a reward for Sammy's success and an indicator that the club expected him to get even better.

"We saw a five-tool player who was coming into what are the prime years for most guys," explained Cubs general manager Ed Lynch. "We were banking that he would continue to improve." And team president Andy McPhail said, "I think Sammy deserves this because of the contributions he has made over the past few years."

The 1997 season continued to be a great one for Sammy. On August 20, he singled off Florida Marlins pitcher Livan Hernandez for his 1,000th big-league hit. Just four days later he hit his 200th big-league home run off Montreal's Steve Kline. With the same swing, he drove in his 100th run of the season, marking the third straight year that he had reached the 100 RBI plateau.

Sammy finished the year with 36 home runs, the seventh-best total in the National League. His 119 RBIs tied his previous best figure, set in 1995, and ranked him sixth in the league. He was one of just four National Leaguers who appeared in every game, and he set a new career high for hits in a season with 161, although his batting average dropped off to just .251. Sammy also flashed his speed on the basepaths, stealing 18 bases.

Defensively, he continued to improve his play in the outfield. In an April 2 game against the Florida Marlins, Sammy threw out two runners with great throws from right field. Sammy had 16 assists from the outfield in 1997, the second-best total in the National League. Base runners had to respect Sammy's arm when they considered whether or not to try for an extra base against the Cubs.

When asked about his improved play, Sammy told reporters, "I worked at it every day at the beginning of the year. When I first came to this team, I was all over the place and made a lot of mistakes. Now I am learning from my mistakes. Right now I am just trying to go out there and be smart. I just try to think about situations before they happen. I believe that I have myself under control, and that is how I want it."

Despite this steady improvement, Sammy still needed to work on many aspects of his game. He needed to become a more patient hitter at the plate. He had struck out 174 times in 1997, leading the league in this category. There were still people who thought that Sammy was more interested in building up his own statistics than helping his team to win games.

When Billy Williams took another coaching position with the Cubs in 1997, the team hired a new batting coach, Jeff Pentland, in the middle of the season. Pentland carefully studied Sammy at the plate. "I always thought this guy could really put up some gigantic numbers if we could get him to swing at better pitches and get him to be more patient," Pentland said after analyzing the slugger. Sammy was swinging at too many pitches that nobody could hit. Pentland's solution? "We needed to come up with some way for him to read and recognize pitches sooner," the coach explained. This would help Sammy refrain from swinging at bad pitches, and hopefully cut down on his strikeouts.

Pentland stressed that Sammy should be patient at the plate and wait for the pitcher to throw him a good pitch to hit. Looking back at the 1997 season, the batting coach had found that Sammy had had 84 one-pitch at-bats. In other words, Sammy had swung at the first pitch and put the ball into play 84 times. Pentland explained to Sosa that a pitcher's first offering to a batter is often not the easiest pitch to handle. If the pitcher falls behind in the count, he is forced to throw strikes, giving the batter a much better pitch to hit. Swinging at the first pitch is a sign of batter impatience; baseball scouts know which

Sammy strikes a humorous pose while dressed as Santa Claus during a photo shoot. During his "Sammy Claus" tour in 1997, he visited underprivileged children in the Dominican Republic and in major U.S. cities, giving away toys and gifts.

players are impatient at the plate and will instruct their team's pitchers to keep their first pitches out of these batters' preferred hitting zones, thereby reducing their effectiveness.

After the season ended, Pentland gave Sosa a videotape showing the swings of three good National League hitters: Chipper Jones of the Atlanta Braves, Sammy's teammate Mark Grace, and Sosa himself. All three tapped their front toes on the ground as they started their swings. But while both Grace and Jones tapped their feet when the pitch was about halfway to the plate, Sammy waited until the ball was almost upon him before he started his swing. As a result, Chipper Jones and Mark Grace each had a fraction of a second more time to decide whether or not to swing than Sammy Sosa did. The benefit of this time was reflected in their statistics: both Jones and Grace struck out far less than Sammy, and each drew more walks.

The slugger got the point. Together, coach and player worked on drills that would help Sammy develop better patience at the plate.

Sammy didn't spend the entire off-season working on his hitting. He had purchased a 60-foot yacht, which he named *Sammy Jr.* after his son, but much of his large contract was dedicated to charity work. He started the Sammy Sosa Charitable Foundation to help disadvantaged children in the Chicago area, explaining, "This foundation is my opportunity to give kids in need a chance at a better life. I was lucky enough to get the chance to play baseball. I want to give less fortunate kids the chance they need." He continued to send money for good causes to the Dominican Republic, and in December he visited Chicago, New York, Washington, Philadelphia, and Miami, delivering toys and gifts to underprivileged children in those cities on his "Sammy Claus World Tour."

He was sorry to hear about the death of longtime Cubs broadcaster Harry Caray. A baseball legend in the broadcast booth, Caray had been a fan favorite at Wrigley Field, leading the singing of "Take Me Out to the Ball Game" in the seventh inning. Caray had been terrible at remembering names and had often called Sammy "Salsa," not Sosa. Sammy didn't mind: it created a great nickname for him.

As Sammy prepared for the 1998 season, working on patience at the plate, Jeff Pentland set two goals. He wanted the slugger to get 100 walks (Sammy's previous high was 58, in 1995) and score 100 runs (he had scored 92 runs in 1993 and 90 runs in '97). Sammy added a third goal—he wanted to bat .300 for the season. That would be quite an improvement, as Sammy's career batting average to that point was just .257. But if he could keep from swinging at bad pitches, it could be done.

"I don't want to go to home plate with the idea that I need to hit a home run," Sammy commented. "I just want to relax and use all the field. When I do that, I know I can hit a home run at any moment."

Sammy Sosa blows a kiss to his mother after a 1998 home run—an image that would become very common that season.

7

ENTERING THE RACE

WHEN SAMMY REPORTED to spring training in 1998, it was obvious to everyone in the Cubs' camp in Mesa, Arizona, that he was ready for a big year. But the eyes of the baseball world were not on the Chicago slugger. Instead, people were focused on what promised to be an exciting assault on one of baseball's most hallowed records: the single-season home-run mark of 61, set by Roger Maris of the New York Yankees in 1961.

No one had come close to 61 homers in the 37 years after Maris set the record. In fact, just hitting 50 home runs in a season is an incredible accomplishment that has been done by only a handful of players. Hank Aaron, baseball's all-time career home run leader with 755, never hit more than 47 in a season. Mike Schmidt, a great slugger for the Philadelphia Phillies in the 1970s and 1980s who led the league in home runs eight times, had a high of 48 in 1980. After Maris's 61, no player broke the 50 mark until George Foster of the Cincinnati Reds hit 52 in 1977. The next to reach the plateau was Detroit's Cecil Fielder in 1990.

But as the 1990s drew to a close, a number of talented sluggers came on the big-league scene. Albert Belle, a temperamental outfielder for the Cleveland Indians, socked 50 homers in 1995. The next year, Seattle Mariners superstar Ken Griffey Jr. made the strongest challenge yet to Maris's record, finishing with 56 home runs. (Griffey's father had been a star with the Reds and Yankees in the 1970s and 1980s, but had never hit more than 14 homers in a single season.) Finishing second that year was an Oakland A's slugger named Mark McGwire, who had hit 52 homers.

In 1997, McGwire and Griffey had battled back and forth for the major-league lead in home runs. Griffey finished with 56 once again, while McGwire ended the year with 58 homers, one of the best figures in baseball history. In fact, he tied three players for the fourth-best single-season total of all time. (However, although Mark McGwire hit more home runs than any other major-league player in 1997, he did not lead either league. The A's, an American League club, had traded him to the St. Louis Cardinals of the National League halfway through the season. McGwire had 34 official American League homers and 24 NL roundtrippers.)

The closest challenge yet to Maris's record prompted sportswriters to predict that 1998 was the year that the home-run record would fall, either to Griffey or to McGwire. And both players started off strong in their pursuit of the mark. Mark hit a home run with the bases loaded (a "grand slam") on the first day of the season, and hit homers in each of his next three games. By the end of April, the first month of the season, both McGwire and Griffey had 11 home runs and were leading their respective leagues.

Sammy was not so concerned about being a part of the home-run race. He was more interested in improving at the plate. On April 4 he pounded an outside pitch from Montreal pitcher Marc Valdes over the ivy-covered wall in Wrigley. "Today I hit a home run to right field that I might have popped up if I tried to pull the ball," he commented afterward. "So our team is doing everything right to win. We're all having fun."

After the first 10 games, the Cubs had a division-leading 8-2 record and Sammy was batting .318 with 9 RBIs. National League pitchers began to realize that Sammy was going to be a lot harder to get out in 1998 than he had been in 1997. By the end of April, Sammy had 6 home runs, 17 RBIs, 7 stolen bases, and was batting .343.

Coaches and friends knew the reason for the change. Chuck Cottier, a friend and former Cubs coach, said to Sammy, "There's a lot of hits in right field, aren't there?" Sammy agreed, telling Cottier, "I believe it now." And Jeff Pentland summed up Sammy's hard work by saying, "I think Sammy has matured with experience. He has a knowledge of the pitchers and has a belief in himself. He believes he can hit the two-strike pitch, so he's not afraid to go to strike two. I think he's matured and gotten confident, and I like the fact that he's gotten patient."

Mark Grace, who batted fourth in the Cubs' regular lineup, just after Sammy, also commented on his new-found patience. "Instead of going up there and trying to hit the first pitch out of the ballpark, he realized that with his talent, he might be able to hit the fourth or fifth pitch out of the park just as easily as the first one," Grace said.

While he was getting a lot of hits, though, Sammy's home-run totals were down from previous years. In mid-May, he only had seven homers in his team's 39 games. As Sammy stood on first base in Colorado's Coors Field after another single, Rockies first baseman Dante Bichette jokingly said, "What? You're not going to hit any more home runs; just going the other way now?" Although Sosa gave no indication that he heard the good-natured ribbing, Bichette then commented, "Don't worry about it. . . . They come in bunches."

Meanwhile, all of baseball's attention was riveted on McGwire and Griffey. On May 19, McGwire hit three home runs in a game at Philadelphia, and by May 25 he had

Sammy rounds the bases during a June game. He catapulted himself into the home-run race that month by hitting a record 20 home runs.

taken the major-league lead with 25. He was on a pace to break the record by a comfortable margin—if he could keep it up. Sammy Sosa, meanwhile, was starting to heat up. He had 11 homers by May 25 and was just going to get hotter.

For the next month, Sammy stole the headlines from Mark McGwire. He homered on his first at-bat of June, and pounded ball after ball over the fences of National League parks for the rest of the month. Sammy finally finished with a roundtripper in his last at-bat of June 1998. When the dust settled, he had set a new record for home runs in a single month, with 20. (The old mark of 18 had been set by Detroit's Rudy York in 1937.) He had also driven in 40 runs. He was the easy choice for National League Player of the Month.

Sammy's power was incredible. He homered eight times during one week (June 14–20), tying Ralph Kiner and two others for the National League record. He homered in five straight games between June 3 and 8. He hit five home runs in three games from June 19–21. But Sammy was not just swinging for the fences and forgetting what Pentland had taught him about patience at the plate. He remained among the league leaders in hitting with a .327 average.

This spectacular month catapulted Sammy into the middle of what sportswriters were calling the Great Home Run Race. On July 1, his 33 homers placed him second in the National League, right behind McGwire's 37 and ahead of the other slugger who had been expected to make a run at the record, Ken Griffey Jr., who had 30 home runs at the midseason All-Star break. Despite the attention this three-way home-run race was getting, however, Sammy's focus was on helping his team win. The Cubs were still in contention for a playoff spot, and making the postseason inspired him more than a home-run duel with Mark McGwire, he told reporters.

Thanks to his improved hitting and his big month of June, Sammy was selected for the 1998 National League All-Star Team. It was the second time he had received this honor. However, his shoulder was bothering him so Sammy opted not to play in the game. He preferred to rest himself for the second half of the season, so that he could help the Cubs make the playoffs.

During the three-day All-Star Break, fans and sportswriters discussed the Great Home Run Race. And Sammy Sosa was one of the most intriguing questions. Could the Dominican slugger with the huge smile keep pace with McGwire and Griffey and make a run at Maris's record in the second half?

Baseball fans all over the country were caught up in the excitement of Mark McGwire and Sammy Sosa's attempt to break the single-season home-run record. These Cubs fans who live over the outfield wall in Wrigley Field even posted a target for their hero Sammy, who was leading the race at the time, 48 home runs to 47 by McGwire.

8

MOST VALUABLE PLAYER

IN 1969, A GREAT HITTER named Reggie Jackson made a strong run at Roger Maris's home-run record. In the first half of the year, he hit an incredible 39 home runs, setting a major-league record. It looked as though there was no way he could fail to break the record. Sportswriters speculated that the Oakland slugger might finish with 75 or 80 homers. However, in the second half of the season Jackson could manage just eight home runs to finish with 47. Not only did he fail to surpass Maris, he did not even break 50.

That was the way that every assault on Maris's record ended for many years. But both Mark McGwire and Sammy Sosa continued going strong in the second half of the season. In July, the first month after the All-Star Break, McGwire pounded eight home runs and Sosa nine. One of these was the first grand slam of Sammy's career. Sosa was responsible for all six Cubs runs that day: he had hit a two-run homer in the sixth inning to tie the game, then the four-bagger with the bases loaded to win it in the eighth. Incredibly, he hit another grand slam the next day. On August 1, Sammy was just three behind

McGwire, 45 to 42. Ken Griffey, meanwhile, had hit his 41st on July 30, but he then went into a slump; he would not hit another home run until late in August.

McGwire commented on the importance of keeping a steady pace. "I've always said—I've been saying it for 11 years now—that the only way anyone's going to hit 62 home runs is if he has at least 50 going into September," he told reporters. "It would be too difficult otherwise. You get close and you don't see many pitches to hit. Every pitcher starts working on you every at-bat."

Pitchers were being especially cautious when either of the two sluggers were at the plate. McGwire was leading the league in walks by a wide margin, and was on pace to challenge Babe Ruth's record of 170 walks in a season. Sammy, too, was walking much more often than he had in the past. Sometimes, pitchers would issue him an intentional pass to first base, just to keep him from hitting a game-breaking home run.

Although the Great Home Run Race was heating up, the two sluggers who had become the focus of attention maintained a polite attitude with the media. They were also very respectful of each other, and their competition was conducted in a spirit of fun and comradeship. "I'm rooting for Mark McGwire," Sammy said at one point. "I look up to him the way a son does to a father. I look at him, the way he hits, the way he acts, and I see the person and the player I want to be. I'm the man in the Dominican Republic. He's the man in the United States. That's the way it should be."

McGwire expressed similar sentiments, telling reporters, "I am extremely happy for Sammy. Sammy is having a magical year. A way better year than I'm having. His team is right there in the wild-card race, he's driven in quite a few more runs than I have, he's hit for a higher average. He's right there. You tip your hat to him."

The two did get involved in a minor controversy during their race when sportswriters learned that McGwire had been taking a testosterone supplement called Androsten-

edione. The substance helps weightlifters build muscle mass, but it does not improve the hand-eye coordination needed to hit home runs. McGwire tried to downplay the reports, pointing out that the substance is not banned by Major League Baseball, and Sosa joked about the situation, telling reporters that he too took pills—Flintstone vitamins—before games.

On August 19, Sammy hit his 48th roundtripper against the Cardinals at Wrigley Field. For the first time all season, he was leading the league in home runs. But Sosa's lead lasted less than an hour. In the 8th inning of the game, McGwire homered to tie the game, then in the 10th he

Fan and media attention were intense during the home-run race of 1998, but both Mark McGwire and Sammy Sosa handled the pressure gracefully. The two sluggers did not even admit a competition for the home-run title; instead, they rooted for each other to be successful. "Imagine if we're tied at the end," McGwire commented at one point. "What a beautiful way to end the season."

blasted his 49th to win the game and retake the lead.

The next day, McGwire hit his 50th of the season. As he rounded the bases, he pumped his fist in the air. He had just become the first player in major-league history to hit 50 homers in three consecutive seasons. Babe Ruth had held the old record, hitting 50 in back-to-back seasons twice in his great career. Sammy soon followed, bashing his 50th of the year on August 23, in the fifth inning of a game against Houston.

By September 1, both men were poised for a run at the record. They were tied at 55 home runs apiece. But while McGwire was supposed to be in the middle of this historic pursuit of Maris, Sosa was putting on the kind of unexpected show that had millions suddenly rooting for him as the underdog. Some Dominicans began painting "SOSA" in white on their car windows as a show of support.

McGwire, it would turn out, would be the first to catch Maris. He hit two homers on September 1 and two more on September 2 to raise his total to 59. Sammy raised his mark to 56 on September 2, then hit his 57th on September 4. That was good enough to break the team record of 56, which had been set by Hack Wilson in 1930. The next day, Sammy hit his 58th while Mark pounded his 60th.

Perhaps destiny was at work, as the Cardinals and Cubs were scheduled for a three-game series in St. Louis's Busch Stadium on September 6–8. On September 7, McGwire tied Maris's record with his 61st homer. The next night, the ballpark was like a carnival. Every time Mark swung at the ball, thousands of flashbulbs went off in the stands like fireworks. In the fourth inning McGwire smashed a pitch from Cubs starter Steve Trachsel that barely cleared the fence in left field.

As the stands erupted in a thunderous ovation, the new home-run champion circled the bases. Sammy ran in from right field to join the Cardinal players who were congratulating Mark at home plate. Sammy waited his turn and then jumped into Mark's arms in a warm embrace.

Sammy stands with his mother, Lucretia, at Sammy Sosa Day in Wrigley Field, September 20, 1998.

The next week would be Sammy's turn to shine. He blasted four home runs, vaulting past Ruth and Maris and tying McGwire for the major-league lead. His 61st and 62nd homers had been hit in the same game, before 40,846 appreciative Cubs fans at Wrigley Field. The crowd went wild with applause; Sammy received a six-minute standing ovation and came out of the dugout three times to respond to the cheers. From St. Louis, McGwire commented, "I think it's awesome. I've said a thousand times that I'm not competing against him. I can only take care of myself. Imagine if we're tied at the end. What a beautiful way to end the season."

The two best sluggers in baseball continued battling through September. After McGwire retook the lead with his 63rd, Sosa tied the race again with a towering grand slam on September 16. The towering eighth-inning shot won the game for the Cubs.

When Sammy failed to get a home run on September 18, a reporter asked him if he was bothered. The Cubs' star shook his head and smiled, saying, "I will go home, have a couple of glasses of wine with my wife and watch Mark hit a home run." This was exactly what happened—McGwire walloped his 64th in a game at Milwaukee that night. He then then hit number 65 on September 20, but three days later Sammy hit two home runs, tying for the lead once again.

On September 25 Sammy became the first major-league baseball player ever to hit 66 home runs in a season when he knocked a pitch from Houston's José Lima out of the park. Once again, his lead lasted just a short time—this time, only 46 minutes—before McGwire tied the race again with his 66th against Montreal.

In the final week of the season, Sammy finally fell off the pace. He went hitless in his next 17 at-bats, while McGwire finished with four homers to set a new record, 70. But what was most important to the Cubs' slugger was that his team was in the middle of a hot race for the wild-card playoff spot with the New York Mets and the San Francisco Giants. When the season ended, Chicago and San Francisco were tied for the wild-card spot. A one-game playoff would decide which team would go to the postseason.

Although Sammy did not hit a home run in the playoff game, he did go 2-for-4 as Chicago beat the Giants, 5 to 3. There was a wild celebration in the clubhouse; the Cubs had reached the playoffs for the first time since 1989.

Unfortunately, their first opponent in the postseason was the powerful Atlanta Braves, winners of 106 games

Spraying champagne, Sammy celebrates the Cubs' victory over San Francisco that clinched the National League wild-card playoff spot in 1998. It was the team's first playoff appearance since 1989. However, the Atlanta Braves, winners of 106 games in the regular season, were too much for Chicago in the first round of the postseason.

during the regular season and boasting a solid lineup and the best pitching staff in the league. The Braves swept the Cubs in three games to advance to the National League Championship Series.

Although he was disappointed at his team's quick playoff exit, Sammy had to be pleased with his statistics. In addition to the 66 home runs, he had led the league with 158 RBIs, the fourth-highest figure in National League history, and batted .308, the highest average of his career. He collected 198 hits, scored 134 runs, and walked 73 times. He hit three homers in a game once and hit two in the same game ten times, setting a new major-league record for multi-homer games.

The slugger was excited when the *Sporting News* announced that he had been named its Player of the Year. In a vote of players, he had received 191 votes; Mark McGwire was second with $185^1/_2$. "That's unbelievable.

I'm very surprised," Sammy commented. "It's a great honor, but especially an honor because it comes from the players who play against me.

"I'm just starting to realize what I did. Now I'm sitting down and watching videos and I'm starting to realize that I hit 66 home runs," he continued. "To tell you the truth, the whole year I only had one thing on my mind and that was to go to the playoffs, and that's what happened. I wasn't worried about the home runs, but now I realize what's happened. Now I sit down and think about it. I hope 66 is there for a long time, but I know someone will have to go through me to get to Mark McGwire at 70."

Just a few weeks later, Sammy received one of baseball's most prestigious awards when he was named the National League's Most Valuable Player, receiving 30 of 32 first-place votes. Although McGwire had also had an incredible year, many sportswriters picked the Cubs' slugger because of his importance in leading his team to the playoffs. Despite McGwire's contribution, the Cardinals barely finished above .500, at 83–79.

"I know McGwire had a great year, but what Sosa did for his club meant a lot more than what McGwire did for his club," summed up *Pittsburgh Post-Gazette* sports writer Paul Meyer. "I kept thinking, 'How do you put McGwire ahead of this guy?'"

Even the highly respected manager of the Cardinals, Tony LaRussa, had indicated during the season that the MVP nod should go to Sammy. "I'm so biased [in favor of McGwire] that it's ridiculous, but I think Sammy deserves it," LaRussa had told reporters in late September. "I don't think he has done more for his team than Mark has, but his team has done more than ours has, so his contribution counts for a little more in my book."

Sammy was just the ninth Cub to win the award, joining such greats as Rogers Hornsby (1929), Ernie Banks (1958 and '59), Ryne Sandberg (1984), and Andre Dawson (1987). Another former Chicago star named Ron

Santo, who was a broadcaster for the team in 1998, felt that Sammy's season was the best ever by a Cub.

"I've never seen a season like this," Santo told the *Chicago Tribune*. "I would say this has to rank, if you look at the MVP awards, as unique. Not only did he put up the numbers—and astronomical numbers—and bring the Cubs to the playoffs, but it was the way he handled himself.

"I don't recall anybody being an ambassador for baseball, even in my days, like Sammy has been. Usually you're an ambassador after you get out of the game. But what Sammy has brought to the table is unique. There's not a lot of players who could handle what Sammy has handled—to go through that kind of pressure, to put up those numbers and to have fun doing it. It takes a very special person. This has to be the best MVP award I've ever seen presented to anybody."

Sammy waves to fans during a ticker-tape parade down New York City's "Canyon of Heroes." The months between the 1998 and 1999 seasons were busy for Sammy; in addition to baseball commitments, he spent a lot of time raising money to help the residents of the hurricane-damaged Dominican Republic.

9
A HELPING HAND

ON SEPTEMBER 22, 1998, just as Sammy Sosa was in the heat of the home-run race with Mark McGwire, a monster storm struck the Dominican Republic. Hurricane Georges pummeled the small country. More than 200 people were killed, and floodwaters destroyed or damaged countless homes. Over 7,000 were left homeless in Santo Domingo alone, and the damage to farms, roads, and buildings was estimated at more than $1.2 billion. Among the towns hardest hit was San Pedro de Macorís. More than a month later, Sammy Sosa's home town still lacked electricity and running water.

Soon after the storm, the president of the Dominican Republic, Leonel Fernández Reyna, telephoned Sammy in Chicago to describe the devastation. Reyna asked Sosa for his help, but he also told him that that the best thing to do was to "play your game." The entire Dominican Republic had been following Sammy's pursuit of McGwire, and his performance was a source of tremendous national pride.

Sosa told Reyna, "I have to do everything I can to help my people, I have to try to find the strength to play a good game tonight." Then he went out and slugged his 66th homer of the year.

Sammy spent the next morning telephoning his family and friends on the island to make sure that they were all right and to see what he could do. By October 15, the Sammy Sosa Foundation had raised nearly $300,000 for relief of the devastation in the Dominican Republic. A lot of people around the country, impressed with Sammy's exploits during the year and wishing to help the people of his homeland, sent contributions. One man from Oklahoma City sent $500, while a lot of people sent $66—$1 for each of Sammy's 1998 home runs. The Cubs donated $50,000 to Sammy's foundation to help the hurricane victims, and Major League Baseball gave $1 million to the American Red Cross for disaster relief in the Dominican Republic and Puerto Rico.

On October 21 Sammy returned to the Dominican Republic on board the Chicago Cubs's jet. It was raining softly when he arrived. President Reyna and baseball Hall of Famer Juan Marichal were among the dignitaries who welcomed Sammy as he came off the airplane in Santo Domingo. "I feel great to be back home," Sammy told the crowd. "Now that I'm here in my country, I have time to go to every corner and barrio to see what the people need. All the people in my country, they believe in me. But I cannot take care of everybody. I want to let them know I'm here, but I'm also a human being."

It took five hours for his motorcade to reach San Pedro de Macorís from the capital. The entire route was lined by thousands of fans, often standing ten deep along the side of the road, who had waited all day in the rain to see Sammy. The baseball star flashed his huge smile and waved to the fans all the way. Uprooted palm trees lay by the side of the road beside broken and crushed billboards. Many of the people in the crowds now only had the clothes on their backs.

When he finally reached his hometown, Sammy was greeted by Mayor Sergio Cedeno of San Pedro de

Macorís. He told Sammy that three planeloads of food and medical supplies had already arrived for the people of the town. With tears in his eyes, Sammy told his hometown fans, "I am proud to be a Dominican. Someday I will give you all that you need. That's something I want to do for San Pedro."

He later told the *Chicago Tribune*, "If I had time, I would be on vacation. But I'm taking care of people in my country. The MVP is great. Sixty-six home runs are great. But when I go home, I know a lot of people don't have anything. No house. Nothing. They only have one hope, and I'm trying to come through for them."

Thanks to his many charitable deeds, as well as his humanitarian efforts following the hurricane, Sammy Sosa received the 1998 Roberto Clemente Man of the Year Award. This award is given each year to a major-league baseball player who balances outstanding skills on the field with civic accomplishments off the diamond.

It would be a busy off-season for Sammy. In addition to traveling around the Dominican Republic, bringing relief supplies and smiles to the people in need, he had found the time to play on an All-Star Team in Japan. While he was there, Sammy and his brother Jose met with members of the Japanese govenment in Tokyo and convinced them to send 1,000 prefabricated housing units to the Dominican Republic. And proving that he had not lost his focus, Sammy hit a homer in the very first game and got to hear yet again the sound of a crowd chanting his name.

It was a sound that never got old. In October 1998 Sammy was given a ticker-tape parade in New York City—an honor usually reserved for astronauts, war heroes, and heads of state. Under a brilliant fall sky, Sammy rode a float up what is called the "Canyon of Heroes," walled in by tall office buildings, to the wild cheers of thousands of fans camped along the streets. Mayor Rudolph Giuliani gave Sammy a key to the city of New York and praised Sammy for his outstanding example to the youth of the

Sammy Sosa joins first lady Hillary Rodham Clinton at the annual State of the Union address delivered by President Clinton in January 1999. Three months earlier, Sammy and Hillary had visited the devastated Dominican Republic together.

world. He called Sammy, "a Dominican hero, an American hero, a hero around the world."

Why do so many people like Sammy Sosa? Perhaps it is because he is almost always smiling. "I've been good with everyone, and I also do my job on the field," he explains. "I handled myself good off the field, and I treated people nice. I make people happy, and they support me 100 percent."

When President Bill Clinton publicly praised Sammy to a national television audience, he focused on Sammy the compassionate human being more than on Sammy the home-run hitter. On January 19, 1999, in the State of the Union Address before the Senators and Representatives of Congress, the President spoke about the devastating hurricane that had struck both the Dominican Republic and the United States. "The American people have opened their arms and their hearts to our Central American and

Caribbean neighbors devastated by recent hurricanes. Working with Congress, we will help them rebuild. . . . Sports records are made, and sooner or later, they are broken. But making other people's lives better—and showing our children the true meaning of brotherhood—that's something that lasts forever. So for far more than baseball, Sammy Sosa, you are a hero of two countries."

Upstairs in the gallery, Sammy sat dressed in a handsome dark suit. He rose proudly to receive a standing ovation from the Senators and Representatives. It was a special, and well-deserved, moment.

Sammy greets spectators and signs autographs before a game. The Dominican slugger's friendly smile and positive attitude have won him fans all over the world.

10

BACK IN THE GROOVE

"I DON'T KNOW IF I can have another year like [the 1998 baseball season]," Sammy Sosa told reporters during spring training for the 1999 baseball season. "But you never know what will happen."

No one could have faulted Sammy if his 1999 season did not measure up to the previous season. After all, few players in major-league history have ever had a better year than Sammy Sosa did in 1998, culminating in his selection as the NL's Most Valuable Player.

He probably could have been chosen the league's Most Popular Player as well, if there were such an award: Sammy's cheerful demeanor during his dogged pursuit of the record had captured the hearts of millions of baseball fans. Mark McGwire himself publicly thanked Sosa for pushing him and making the race fun. Sosa's teammates loved him, too—he'd inspired them to play some of the best baseball seen in Wrigley Field in many years, as the Cubs made the playoffs for the first time since 1989.

So after a magical year like 1998, it would be understandable for Sammy to let down a little bit. He received a hero's welcome when he reported for Chicago's spring training in Mesa, Arizona, on March 1, 1999. "People lined up for his autograph," wrote sports reporter Rick Gano. "Everyone basked in his huge smile."

Early in the 1999 season, it appeared several players might set the home run pace for the new season, although it seemed unlikely that anyone would break McGwire's record. The Cardinals' slugger remained the best bet to lead the majors in home runs, and he did not disappoint, hitting a roundtripper in his club's season opener. Two other sluggers, Tampa Bay's Jose Canseco and Seattle's Ken Griffey Jr., also hit home run after home run early in the season.

Sammy Sosa started out more slowly. He didn't hit a home run until the Cubs's sixth game, on April 11, 1999. For a time, it looked like Sosa might not even hit 50 home runs over the season. After hitting his fourth homer in his 15th game, he did not hit another for nearly two weeks. In late April and early May, the entire Cubs' lineup failed to get any home runs in eight straight games. But then things changed for the better. On May 4, five Cubs hit homers, and Sammy's two-run blast that day seemed to start him on a roll. He followed with home runs on May 5, 8, 11, and 14. Then on May 17, he hit two in one game. He hit six more by the end of the month, including one on May 28 when the Cubs faced Mark McGwire's St. Louis Cardinals for the first time in 1999. Two hundred fifty media representatives attended that game.

With his bat coming alive, and his play in the field solid, Sammy was named the National League's Player of the Month for May. His importance to the team was obvious: during April, as Sammy struggled, the team was just 10–10, but as his bat came alive in May the Cubs did too, posting a record of 17–10 for the month.

At the start of June, Sammy Sosa had 16 home runs for the season; McGwire, surprisingly, had just 13, and wasn't even the leading home-run hitter on his own team. Raul Mondesi of the Los Angeles Dodgers was leading the

National League in homers, and American Leaguers Jose Canseco and Ken Griffey Jr. had each hit more roundtrippers than Sammy. But on June 3, Sosa took over the National League's home-run lead in a 7-2 win over the San Diego Padres.

The next day, the Cubs beat the Cleveland Indians to raise their record to 30–21. Unfortunately, this would be the high point of the season for Chicago. By the end of June, their record stood at 37–37; they had fallen five games under .500 (48–53) by July 31, then suffered through a horrible August, going 6–24 for the month.

Despite the team's troubles, Sammy continued to hit home runs. On June 26 he belted a sixth-inning pitch from Philadelphia hurler Robert Person out of the park for his 300th career homer. But Sammy was disappointed that his 27th home run of the season did not help his team against the Phillies, as the Cubs lost, 6–2. "I can enjoy having my 300th home run, but not in a loss," he said afterward. "I know it's a good accomplishment and I feel lucky to have hit so many home runs. But I'm not through yet. Hopefully there will be more records but more importantly, more wins for our team."

In July Sammy Sosa was selected to the All-Star Team for the third time—his first time as a starter. In the last week of voting for the All-Stars, fans had cast one million votes for Sammy. He went hitless in the game.

By August, Jose Canseco was on the injured list and Griffey's production had fallen off. Meanwhile, Mark McGwire had finally heated up and fans realized they were going to see another race between McGwire and Sosa for the National League home-run crown. McGwire homered in 15 of the first 19 games after the All-Star Break, catching Sammy with number 40 on August 1. The two players remained even, belting two homers apiece over the next four days, before McGwire pulled ahead on August 6 when he hit a pair of home runs. The first was a milestone for the St. Louis slugger, his 500th career

Sammy was such a fan favorite that he received more All-Star votes than any other National League player in 1999. Here, he is standing with Seattle superstar Ken Griffey Jr., a great slugger in his own right and the leading vote-getter for the American League All-Star Team.

homer, and it gave him 44 for the season, two ahead of Sammy's 42.

But Sammy did not give up. On August 20, he recovered the lead when he hit two homers, his 48th and 49th. And by the middle of September, Sosa had pulled ahead, with 59 home runs to McGwire's 56.

When Sosa hit his 60th home run on September 18, the Wrigley Field crowd cheered wildly. A day later, Slammin' Sammy hit 61 as his youngest son, Michael, watched from the stands at Wrigley Field. Sosa said later that Michael, who was celebrating his second birthday, really didn't understand why the stadium erupted after his father slammed the ball over the outfield wall. "Right now, he just likes to be around daddy," Sosa said.

The day after Sosa hit 61, McGwire hit his 57th and 58th. On September 20–22, the Cubs hosted the Cardinals for a three-game series. In the first game, McGwire hit his 59th homer of the season, breaking up a bid for a perfect game by Chicago pitcher Jon Lieber in the seventh inning and sparking a 7-2 St. Louis victory. "It was a great game," Sammy said after picking up a single and a walk in four plate appearances. "Lieber pitched a great game. . . . He was making perfect pitches and dominated the game until the seventh inning. It was a great game for both sides."

The next two games of the series were not great for either slugger. Neither one managed to homer; in fact, neither could manage a hit, going a combined 0-for-17.

Sammy had cooled down significantly at the plate in September. Over the first five months of the season, he had batted .302; in September, he struggled to just a .234 average with only 7 home runs and 17 RBIs. He still had an outside chance to tie Mark McGwire's 1998 record of 70 home runs, but it would take a great power surge: nine home runs in the team's last 10 games.

McGwire contined to put the pressure on; he tied Sammy with his 61st homer on September 27. The next day Sosa hit his 62nd of the season, and the Wrigley Field crowd went wild once again. Fans were amazed that the slugger had been able to concentrate, for earlier that day his wife had been admitted to the hospital because of an adverse reaction to prescription medication. After the game Sosa assured the press that his wife was okay. That meant, he said, "I had to go out and do my job."

On September 29 McGwire caught and passed Sosa when he pounded two homers, his 62nd and 63rd. With three games left in the season, it was clear that neither player would challenge McGwire's 1998 mark of 70. But the Cardinals and Cubs were matched up for the final series of the year, ensuring a dramatic showdown in the National League home-run race.

Neither player homered in the first game of the series, but McGwire extended his lead to two with his 64th of the year on October 2. For the final game of the season, the

Sammy was the recipient of the National League's Hank Aaron Award in 1999, a new award given to the best hitter in each league—one more trophy he could add to a growing collection.

president of the Dominican Republic, Leonel Fernández Reyna, showed up to throw out the first pitch. In the first inning, McGwire belted his 65th of the year, although Sosa pulled back to within two with his 63rd of the year, a three-run shot, in the third inning. It didn't help the team much, though, as the Cubs lost, 9-5, to end a disappointing season with a 67–95 record, last in the NL Central. The Cardinals' year was not much better, as they finished 21 1/2 games out of first place with a 75–86 record.

"[Sammy] had an absolutely wonderful year," McGwire commented afterward. "I think both our our years were obviously very difficult because of what happened with both teams not doing so well."

Despite his late-season slump, Sammy finished with 180 hits, the second-highest total of his career, and a .288 average. He walked 78 times (a new career high), rapped 24 doubles, scored 114 runs, and had 141 RBIs, second best in the National League.

His 63 homers were the fourth-best total in major-league baseball history. Six times he had delighted fans by hitting two homers in one game. No one else in major league baseball had even come close to the home-run numbers posted by McGwire and Sosa. Ken Griffey Jr. had led the American League with 48 homers, and Chipper Jones of the Atlanta Braves had been third in the National League with 45.

On October 4, Sammy Sosa was named the first winner of the National League's Hank Aaron Award, presented to the best hitter in each league. And on the same day, the Cubs announced that Sammy had helped the team set a new record for attendance. Despite the team's poor performance, Cubs fans had turned out in record numbers: attendance at games at Wrigley Field averaged 36,075. A total of 2.81 million people went through the venerable Chicago ballpark's turnstiles in 1999, and most people credited this great attendance to Sammy Sosa.

For Sosa, all that was left was to go home and prepare for the next season. "I am a happy man, not disappointed." said Sosa. "I had a great year. For me, that's something to be happy about."

The slugger also seemed to be looking forward to another home-run derby with Mark McGwire. The Cubs and Cardinals were scheduled to meet in the first week of the next season. "I'm going to go home and relax and work hard to get ready to come back for the year 2000," he said. "I hope that next year we can both have another great year."

CHRONOLOGY

1968   Born November 12 in San Pedro de Macorís, Dominican Republic, to Lucretia and Bautista Montero Sosa

1975   Father Bautista dies in a work accident

1979   Meets American businessman Bill Chase, who helps the Sosa family

1984   Signs baseball contract with the Philadelphia Phillies; contract is voided because at age 15 Sammy is too young.

1985   Signs professional contract with the Texas Rangers for $3,500 bonus

1986   Makes professional baseball debut with Sarasota in the Gulf Coast League; hits .275 with 19 doubles and steals 11 bases in 61 games

1987   Plays with Gastonia in the South Atlantic League and bats .279

1989   Debuts with the Texas Rangers on June 16, and gets first big-league hit; hits first major-league home run on June 21 off Roger Clemens; traded to the Chicago White Sox on July 29; debuts with White Sox August 22 and goes 3-for-3 with a home run

1990   In first full season, hits 15 home runs and drives in 70 runs in 153 games; builds a house for his mother in the Dominican Republic

1991   Because of poor start, demoted to the minor leagues on July 19; returns to White Sox on August 27; finishes season with .203 batting average and 10 home runs in 116 games with Chicago; marries Sonia Esther in November

1992   Traded to the Chicago Cubs on March 30; suffers a broken ankle August 7, ending his season on the disabled list with a .260 batting average in 67 games

1993   Works with Cubs batting coach Billy Williams on swing; named National League Player of the Week (June 28–July 4) for the first time in his career; becomes the first Cub to join the "30–30 club," finishing with 36 stolen bases and 33 home runs

1994   Hits .300 with 25 home runs and 70 RBIs in strike-shortened season

1995   Signs one-year, $4 million contract with the Cubs; named to the National League All-Star Team for the first time; hits 100th career home run in July; sets new career highs in home runs (36) and RBIs (119); signs two-year, $10 million contract with the Cubs

1996   Leading the league in home runs with 40 on August 20, when he is hit in the wrist by a pitch, causing a season-ending injury; finances construction of the 30-30 Plaza, a shopping center in the Dominican Republic

1997　Signs four-year, $42.5 million contract with the Cubs in June; collects both 1,000th career hit and 200th career home run in August; creates Sammy Sosa Charitable Foundation to help disadvantaged children in the Chicago area; visits children in major cities in the United States and the Dominican Republic on his "Sammy Claus World Tour" in December

1998　Sets major-league record with 20 home runs in June; selected to the All-Star Team for the second time; breaks team record with 57th home run on September 4; takes lead in home-run race with 66th home run on September 25; finishes with the second-highest single-season home-run total in major-league history; named National League's Most Valuable Player; raises money to help the victims of Hurricane Georges in the Dominican Republic

1999　Helps Cubs set a team record for attendance, drawing more than 2.8 million fans to Wrigley Field; engages in another home-run race with Mark McGwire and finishes with 63, two behind the St. Louis slugger

APPENDIX

CHARITABLE FOUNDATIONS

The Sammy Sosa Charitable Foundation
c/o The Chicago Cubs
1060 West Addison Street
Chicago, IL 60613
Phone: (773) 404-CUBS
E-mail: comments@mail.cubs.com

The Atkinson Charitable Foundation
One Yonge Street, Fifth Floor
Toronto, Ontario M5E 1E5
Phone: (416) 368-5152
Fax: (416) 865-3619
E-mail: cpascal@thestar.ca

Edyth Bush Charitable Foundation
199 E. Welbourne Avenue
PO Box 1967
Winter Park, FL 32790-1967
Phone: (407) 647-4322
Fax: (407) 647-7716
E-mail: edyth@aol.com

National Children's Leukemia Foundation
233 Broadway, Suite 818
New York, NY 10279
Phone: (212) 587-7474
Fax: (212) 587-7476
E-mail: leukemia@erols.com

Juvenile Diabetes Foundation
120 Wall Street
New York, NY 10005
Phone: (212) 785-9500
Toll-Free: (800) JDF-CURE
Fax: (212) 785-9595
E-mail: info@jdfcure.org

Child Welfare League of America
440 First Street NW, Third Floor
Washington, D.C. 20001-2085
Phone: (202) 638-2952
Fax: (202) 638-4004
Web address: www.cwla.org

Autism Society of America
7910 Woodmart Avenue, Suite 650
Bethesda, MD 20814
Phone: (301) 657-0881
Toll-Free: (800) 3AUTISM
Fax: (301) 657-0869
Web site: www.autism–society.org

Children's Cancer Foundation
PO Box 60012
Arcadia, CA 91066
Phone: (626) 447-1674
Toll-Free: (800) 458-NCCF
Fax: (626) 447-6359

Feed the Children
PO Box 36
Oklahoma City, OK 73101
Phone: (405) 942-0228
Toll-Free: (800) 627-4556
Fax: (405) 945-4177
E-mail: ftc@feedthechildren.org

Pediatric AIDS Foundation
2950 Thirty-First Street, Suite 125
Santa Monica, CA 90404
Phone: (310) 314-1459
Fax: (310) 314-1469
E-mail: info@pedaids.org

Save the Children Federation, Inc.
54 Wilton Road
Westport, CT 06880
Phone: (203) 221-4676
Toll-Free: (800) 243-5075
Web site: www.savethechildren.org

National Center for Learning Disabilities
381 Park Avenue South, Suite 1401
New York, NY 10016
Phone: (212) 545-7510
Toll-Free: (888) 575-7373
Fax: (212) 545-9665
Web site: www.ncld.org

APPENDIX

SAMMY SOSA'S BASEBALL STATISTICS

Year	Team	G	AB	R	H	2B	3B	HR	RBI	BB	SB	AVG
1989	Tex	25	84	8	20	3	0	1	3	0	0	.238
1989	ChiSox	33	99	19	27	5	0	3	10	11	7	.273
	1989 Total	58	183	27	47	8	0	4	13	11	7	.257
1990	ChiSox	153	532	72	124	26	10	15	70	33	32	.233
1991	ChiSox	116	316	39	64	10	1	10	33	14	13	.203
1992	ChiCubs	67	262	41	68	7	2	8	25	19	15	.260
1993	ChiCubs	159	598	92	156	25	5	33	93	38	36	.261
1994	ChiCubs	105	426	59	128	17	6	25	70	25	22	.300
1995	ChiCubs	144	564	89	151	17	3	36	119	58	34	.268
1996	ChiCubs	124	498	84	136	21	2	40	100	34	18	.273
1997	ChiCubs	162	642	90	161	31	4	36	119	45	22	.251
1998	ChiCubs	159	643	134	198	20	0	66	158	73	18	.308
1999	ChiCubs	162	625	114	180	24	2	63	141	78	7	.288
Totals		**1409**	**5289**	**841**	**1413**	**206**	**35**	**336**	**941**	**428**	**224**	**.267**

Babe Ruth takes a mighty swing. The New York Yankees' star was the greatest player in baseball history, batting .342 with 714 home runs over 22 seasons.

APPENDIX

BABE RUTH

On the last day of the 1927 season, the New York Yankees played a meaningless game against the Washington Senators. It was meaningless because the powerhouse Yankees had easily defeated nearly everyone they played, winning 109 games. New York would go on to defeat the Senators and set a major-league record for victories in a season with 110.

But when the Yankees' star player, Babe Ruth, stepped up to the plate that day, a tension gripped the crowd. And when Ruth ripped a pitch from Tom Zachary deep into the stands, the fans in attendance cheered wildly. Ruth had just become the first player to hit 60 home runs in a season.

George and Kate Ruth never dreamed their son would become the greatest player in baseball history. George Herman Ruth Jr. was born on February 6, 1895, in Baltimore, Maryland. Because both of his parents worked, young George was often left alone. When he got into trouble, his parents sent him to a school for delinquent children, St. Mary's Industrial School for Boys, when he was just 7 years old. Babe stayed at St. Mary's for the next 12 years. Through the guidance of Brother Matthias, one of the school's administrators, George found he had a natural talent for baseball. He could whack the ball farther and throw it harder than anyone at St. Mary's had ever seen.

When George was 19, he signed a contract with Jack Dunn, the owner of a team in the minor leagues, the Baltimore Orioles. Thanks to his youth, during his first spring training in March 1914 he received the nickname that he would keep all his life: Babe.

Although he could always hit the ball well, Babe Ruth started his career as a pitcher. He won his first game for the Orioles in 1914 by a shutout, 6–0. But even though people were coming out to see the young Orioles lefthander pitch, the team was not doing well financially. Dunn was forced to sell his young star to the Boston Red Sox, a team in the American League.

The day after Babe Ruth's contract was purchased by the Red Sox, he started his first major-league game, beating the Cleveland Indians, 4–3. He won another game that year, and also got his first big-league hit on October 2, 1914.

The next season, Ruth emerged as one of the Red Sox's best pitchers, winning 18 games and losing just 8 as the team won the World Series. He also belted his first home run, on May 6, but few people noticed, even though home runs were fairly uncommon. At that time, no American League batter had ever hit more than 16 in a season.

Babe Ruth concentrated on pitching, rather than hitting, for the next two years. In 1916 the Red Sox again reached the World Series, and Ruth led the way with a 23–12 record and a 1.75 ERA. In the Series against the Chicago Cubs, Babe won three games and set a major-league record by pitching $29^{2/3}$ consecutive shutout innings.

Boston finished second in the league in 1917. Babe was just as effective, going 24–13 with a 2.01 ERA. The 1918 season was shortened because of World War I, but Babe still went 13–7 with a 2.22 ERA. That season, though, he played 75 games in the outfield on days when he wasn't pitching. He batted .300 and pounded 11 home runs, which tied him for the league lead.

The next year Babe spent more time playing the outfield and less as a pitcher. In 17 games, he compiled a 9–5 record and 2.97 ERA. But it was his hitting that drew the most notice. Babe shattered all records by blasting 29 home runs. (By contrast, the rest of the Boston team hit just four home runs; the National League home-run leader, Gavvy Cravath of the Philadelphia Phillies, hit 12). Babe hit .322, drove in 114 runs, and scored 103.

Despite this, the Red Sox had finished in sixth place, and team owner Harry Frazee was tired of losing games and money. In the off-season, he sold Babe Ruth's contract to the New York Yankees for $125,000.

With the Yankees, the Babe blossomed into the greatest slugger in baseball history. In 1920 he shattered his own record by hitting an incredible 54 home runs—more than any other *team* in the league—batting .376, and drawing 148 walks. He improved his batting average to .378 and his home-run total to 59 the next year, leading the Yankees to their first pennant. Although the team lost the Series in 1921, then lost again in 1922, on the strength of Ruth's bat the Yankees would become the most dominant team of the 1920s and 1930s. New York had many great players, among them Lou Gehrig, Bob Meusel, and Tony Lazzeri, but everyone knew that Babe Ruth was the star.

Babe was one of the most famous people in America. Children lined railroad tracks to see his train rush by. Banks closed when the Babe came to town to play. Newspapers ran a special column, "What Babe Ruth Did Today." Ruth negotiated the highest salary in baseball, $80,000 a year. When a reporter asked Babe how he could justify earning more than the president of the United States, Herbert Hoover, he replied. "I had a better year."

From 1919 through 1931, Babe led the league in homers 12 times, and he hit a record 60 in 1927. This record would stand untouched for 34 years, until Roger Maris, playing in a season that was eight games longer than when Babe had played, broke it by one. Ruth finished with 714 career home runs, a mark that was considered unbreakable until Hank Aaron passed it in 1974. Ruth batted .342 for his career with 2,211 RBIs.

After the 1934 season, Babe Ruth left the Yankees for the Boston Braves. His skills were declining, though, and he only played in 28 games, hitting six home runs but batting just .181. During a Memorial Day doubleheader, he walked off the field and never played again. He was a national icon, however, and fans reacted with shock to the news in 1948 that Babe Ruth was sick with cancer. On August 16, 1948, the greatest player in baseball history died in a Florida hospital.

Roger Maris crosses home plate after pounding a ball out of the park during the 1961 season. He is congratulated by his close friend and teammate Mickey Mantle, who competed with Maris for the home-run crown that season.

APPENDIX

THE 1961 HOME-RUN RACE

Before the 1961 season, the newly hired manager of the New York Yankees, Ralph Houk, felt his team had the potential to be very good. He had no way of knowing that his Yankees team of 1961 would one day be considered among the best of all time, or that two of his star players would engage in an incredible competition to break one of the sport's most hallowed records: Babe Ruth's 60 home runs, set in 1927.

The year before, the Yankees had won the American League pennant but lost to the Pittsburgh Pirates in a seven-game World Series. New York was led by one of the game's superstars, outfielder Mickey Mantle, and had a great lineup that included catcher Yogi Berra, Elston Howard, and Bill Skowron. And a young player named Roger Maris, who had joined the team the year before, was also expected to contribute.

Roger Maris was born on September 10, 1934, in Hibbing, Minnesota. He grew up in in Fargo, North Dakota, where he played both baseball and football in high school. He turned down a football scholarship to the University of Oklahoma to play professional baseball with the Cleveland Indians. After playing a few years on Cleveland farm teams, Maris was traded to Kansas City in 1957. The Yankees traded for him in December 1959, thinking his bat could add the kind of power they needed. They were right. By the end of the year, Roger had won the 1960 American League Most Valuable Player award by batting .283 with 39 home runs and a league-leading 112 RBIs.

During the season, Mantle and Maris became good friends off the field. The older player had learned how to handle the New York press, and he tried to protect Maris, who mistrusted the press and the New York fans.

Maris started out the 1961 season slowly. He did not hit the ball out of the park for nearly a month, finally getting his first homer on April 26. That same day, Mantle hit two home runs to increase his season total to seven.

But Maris started getting hot in May. By the end of the month, he had 11 home runs to Mantle's 13. He passed the Yankees' star by hitting 15 home runs in June, but Mantle came back in July. By July 18, both players had 35 home runs and were 17 games ahead of Ruth's 1927 record-setting pace.

By now sportswriters across the country were eagerly following the race. The attention was very distracting. Some people did not want to see Babe Ruth's record fall. Others were rooting for Mantle, a longtime Yankee hero, to beat Maris, a relative newcomer. The intense pressure began to get to Maris, and both the press and the fans turned against Maris for his surly remarks. Roger's hair started to fall out in clumps. He refused all interviews and sat off by himself on the bench. But he did keep on hitting the ball over the fence.

At the start of September, Maris had 53 homers and Mantle had 48. Mickey Mantle was suffering from injuries that made it hard for him to play, however, and he fell off the pace. But Maris continued to hit home runs. In the 154th game of the season, he hit his 59th homer. When Babe Ruth had set his mark in 1927, the baseball season was 154 games long. By 1961, however, the season had been stretched to 162 games. Four games later, Maris tied the record with his 60th of the year. And in the final game of the season, a Red Sox rookie pitcher named Tracy Stallard served up a fourth-inning pitch that Maris blasted out of the park to set a new major-league record.

It had been a great season for the Yankees, who won 109 games and beat the Cincinnati Reds in the World Series. Mantle had finished the year with 54 home runs, the highest total ever for a runner-up. And Maris, who had led the league in runs (132) and RBIs (142) as well as home runs, was named Most Valuable Player for the second year in a row.

But the home-run race took an emotional toll on Roger Maris. It was hard for many fans to accept that the immortal Babe Ruth's record had been broken. Many pointed to the fact that Maris had needed more games to break the record. In fact, the commissioner of baseball, Ford C. Frick, determined that Maris's accomplishment should have a separate mention in the sport's official record book because of the differential in games played between Maris and the baseball icon.

And even though he was one of just a handful of players ever to win back-to-back MVP awards, Maris never achieved his full potential, or even came close to another year like his 1960 and 1961 seasons. He hit 33 homers and drove in 100 runs in 1962; injuries limited him to 90 games and 23 homers the following season. His last productive year was 1964, when he pounded 26 homers. Although he remained in the league for four more seasons, he hit just 35 more home runs in his career.

Roger Maris would later comment, "It would have been a . . . lot more fun if I had never hit those 61 home runs. All it brought me was headaches." He died on December 14, 1985, in Houston, Texas.

FURTHER READING

Bamberger, Micheal, "Sammy: You're the Man," *Sports Illustrated* 89, no. 13 (28 September 1998): 44–50.

Bjarkman, Peter C. *Baseball with a Latin Beat.* Jefferson, NC: McFarland and Company, 1994.

Chass, Murray. "It's not Easy, but the Cubs find their Way into the Post-Season," *New York Times* (29 September 1998): Section D, p. 1.

Cockcroft, James D. *Latinos in Beisbol: The Hispanic Experience in the Americas.* New York: Franklin Watts, 1996.

Dedman, Bill. "Unlikely Season of Dreams for Cubs." *New York Times* (29 September 1998); Section D, p. 3.

Duncan, P. J. *Sosa: Baseball's Home Run Hero.* New York: Simon and Schuster, 1998.

Goddard, Joe. "Chicago Cubs." *Sporting News* 219, no. 23 (5 June 1995): 21.

Green, Stephen. "Sammy Sosa." *Sports Illustrated* 88, no. 52 (29 June 1998): 41–50.

Gutman, Bill. *Sammy Sosa: A Biography.* New York: Pocket Books, 1998.

Kindred, Dave. "Valuables and Variables." *Sporting News* 222, no. 39 (28 September 1998): 86.

Klein, Alan M. *Sugarball: The American Game, the Dominican Dream.* New Haven: Yale University Press, 1991.

Knisley, Michael, and Steve Marantz. "A Finish with a Flourish." *Sporting News* 222, no. 40 (5 October 1998): 44–48.

Krich, John. *El Beisbol: Travels through the Pan-American Pastime.* New York: Atlantic Monthly Press, 1990.

Muskat, Carrie. *Sammy Sosa.* Childs, MD: Mitchell Lane Publishers, 1999

———. "Sosa's hometown is cash-strapped." *USA Today* (22 October 1998): section C, p. 5.

———. "Hero's return: His country's 'great gift,' in baseball and beyond," *USA Today* (21 October 1998): section A, p. 1.

Oleksak, Michael, and Mary Adams Oleksak. *Beisbol: Latin Americans and the Grand Old Game.* Grand Rapids, MI: Masters Press, 1991.

Rozner, Barry, and Mark Bonavita. "TSN's Baseball Awards," *Sporting News* 222, no. 43 (26 October 1998): 10–11.

Schlossberg, Dan. *The New Baseball Catalog.* Middle Village, NY: Jonathan David Publishers, 1998.

Stein, Joel. "Grand Sam." *Time* 152, no. 13 (28 September 1998): 76–77.

Verducci, Tom. "What a Season," *Sports Illustrated* 89, no. 14 (5 October 1998): 41–52.

INDEX

Aaron, Hank, 59
Alou, Felipe, 21, 27
Alou, Jesus, 21
Alou, Matty, 21
Alvarez, Wilson, 33
American Red Cross, 76
Androstenedione, 66-67
Atlanta Braves, 70-71

Baines, Harold, 33
Banks, Ernie, 72
Bell, George, 39
Belle, Albert, 54, 60
Bere, Jason, 11
Bichette, Dante, 61
Bonds, Barry, 54
Boston Red Sox, 31
Brown, Kevin, 29

Canseco, Jose, 82, 83
Caray, Harry, 57
Caribbean World Series, 30
Cedeno, Sergio, 76
Chase, Bill, 21
Chicago Cubs, 11, 13-14, 39-40, 43, 45, 46, 47, 48, 49, 53, 54, 55, 57, 59, 61, 63, 65, 68, 69, 70, 72, 76, 81, 82, 84-86, 87
Chicago Tribune, 73, 77
Chicago White Sox, 33, 35, 37, 39, 40
Cincinnati Reds, 12, 60, 59
Clemens, Roger, 31
Clemente, Roberto, 20, 40, 48
Cleveland Indians, 60, 83
Clinton, Bill, 78-79
Club Sammy, 50
Colorado Rockies, 61
Congress, U.S., 78

Consuelo, Dominican Republic, 17
Cottier, Chuck, 61
Cox, Bobby, 49

Dawson, Andre, 40, 41, 72
Detroit Tigers, 40
Dinzey, Amado, 22
Dominican Republic, 17, 18, 20, 22, 23, 27, 36, 41, 46, 49, 50, 53, 57, 66, 86
  and Hurricane Georges, 75-77, 78

Fielder, Cecil, 59
Fletcher, Scott, 33
Florida Marlins, 49, 54
Florida State League, 29
Foster, George, 59

Gano, Rick, 82
Gastonia, North Carolina, 27, 29
Giuliani, Rudolph, 77
Gonzalez, Juan, 29
Grace, Mark, 13, 41, 56, 61
"Great Home Run Race, The," 63, 66
Griffey, Ken, Sr., 60
Griffey, Ken, Jr., 60, 61, 63, 66, 82, 83, 87
Grissom, Marquis, 12
Guillen, Ozzie, 36-37
Gulf Coast League, 27

Haiti, 17
Hank Aaron Award, 87
Hawkins, Andy, 30
Hernandez, Livan, 54
Himes, Larry, 39
Hispaniola, 17

Hornsby, Rogers, 72
Houston Astros, 48-49
Hriniak, Walt, 37, 39
Hurricane Georges, 75-77, 78
Hutton, Mark, 49

Jackson, Reggie, 65
Japan, 77
Jones, Chipper, 56, 87

Kiner, Ralph, 63
Klein, Robert, 36
Kline, Steve, 54

LaRussa, Tony, 72
Lefebvre, Jim, 14, 40
Lieber, Jon, 85
Lima, José, 70
Llenas, Winston, 19
Los Angeles Dodgers, 82
Lynch, Ed, 54

McGwire, Mark, 11, 14, 60, 61-62, 63, 65, 66-70, 71, 75, 81, 82, 83-86, 87
McPhail, Andy, 48, 54
Manrique, Fred, 33
Marichal, Juan, 20-21, 76
Maris, Roger, 11, 59, 60, 63, 65, 68, 69
Meyer, Paul, 72
Milwaukee Brewers, 11, 12-14
Minaya, Omar, 22-23, 29
Minnesota Twins, 35
Mondesi, Raul, 82
Montreal Expos, 27

New York City, 77
New York Mets, 70

New York Yankees, 30, 59, 60
Nicaragua, 20

Oakland A's, 60
Oklahoma City 89ers, 32

Patterson, Ken, 39
Pentland, Jeff, 55-56, 57, 63
Person, Robert, 83
Philadelphia Phillies, 22, 59, 83
Pittsburgh Pirates, 40
Pittsburgh Post-Gazette, 72
Port Charlotte, Florida, 29, 30
Puerto Rico, 17, 29, 76

Reyna, Leonel Fernández, 75, 76, 86
Riggleman, Jim, 14, 47
Roberto Clemente Man of the Year Award, 77
Ruth, Babe, 66, 68, 69

St. Louis Cardinals, 11, 60, 67, 68, 72, 82, 84-86, 87
"Sammy Claus World Tour," 57
Sammy Jr., 56
Sammy Sosa Charitable Foundation, 56-57, 76
Sammy Sosa Escuela de Beisbol, 50-51
Sandberg, Ryne, 72
San Diego Padres, 83
San Francisco Giants, 70
San Pedro de Macorís, Dominican Republic, 17, 18, 19, 21, 22, 49-50, 75, 76-77

Santo, Ron, 72-73
Santo Domingo, Dominican Republic, 30, 37, 75, 76
Schmidt, Mike, 59
Scott, Mike, 29
Seattle Mariners, 60
Sosa, Bautista Montero (father), 17, 18
Sosa, José (brother), 19, 77
Sosa, Lucretia (mother), 17, 18-19, 23, 25, 30, 36, 46
Sosa, Michael (son), 84
Sosa, Samuel Peralta
  and All-Star Game, 47, 49, 63, 83
  and baseball school, 50-51
  birth, 17
  charity work, 49-50, 56-57, 75-79
  childhood, 15-23
  education, 19
  injuries, 41, 49
  visits Japan, 77
  major league career, 11-15, 30-32, 33, 35-37, 39-87
  marriage, 37-39
  minor league career, 23, 25-30, 32-33, 35, 37
  wins National League's Most Valuable Player award, 72-73, 77, 81
  given New York City ticker tape parade, 77-78
  and 1998 home run title, 13, 14, 59-73, 75
  and 1999 home run title, 11-15, 81-87
  hits over sixty home runs for second year, 11-15, 84
  joins "30-30" club, 45, 46
  and 30-30 Plaza shopping center, 49-50
  traded to Chicago Cubs, 39
  traded to Chicago White Sox, 33, 39
  and winter ball, 27, 30, 41, 53
Sosa, Sammy, Jr. (son), 51, 56
Sosa, Sonia Esther (wife), 37-39, 41, 46, 51, 70, 85
South Atlantic League, 29
Sporting News, 48, 71
State of the Union Address, 78
Sterling, Hector, 21, 22

Texas League, 30
Texas Rangers, 22, 23, 30-32, 33, 39
  farm teams, 26-30, 32
Tolentino, Juan Francisco, 50
Torres, Jaime, 36
Tulsa Drillers, 30

University of Santo Domingo, 21

Valdes, Marc, 60
Vancouver Canadians, 33, 37

Williams, Billy, 43, 48, 55
Wilson, Hack, 68

York, Rudy, 63

PICTURE CREDITS

page

2:	AP/Wide World Photos	37:	AP/Wide World Photos	67:	AP/Wide World Photos
10:	AP/Wide World Photos	38:	© Ron Vesely	69:	© David Durochik
12:	AP/Wide World Photos	42:	AP/Wide World Photos	71:	CORBIS
13:	AP/Wide World Photos	44:	© David Durochik	74:	AP/Wide World Photos
16:	CORBIS	45:	© David Durochik	78:	AP/Wide World Photos
18:	AP/Wide World Photos	50:	AP/Wide World Photos	80:	© David Durochik
20:	AP/Wide World Photos	52:	© David Durochik	84:	CORBIS
24:	Bill Speer/Silver Image	56:	CORBIS	86:	AP/Wide World Photos
31:	© Ron Vesely	58:	© David Durochik	92:	© David Durochik
32:	AP/Wide World Photos	62:	© David Durochik	94:	CORBIS
34:	© Ron Vesely	64:	© David Durochik	98:	AP/Wide World Photos

ANN G. GAINES has written a dozen nonfiction books for children and young adults. She lives with her husband and four children near Gonzales, Texas.

JAMES SCOTT BRADY serves on the board of trustees with the Center to Prevent Handgun Violence and is the vice chairman of the Brain Injury Foundation. Mr. Brady served as assistant to the president and White House press secretary under President Ronald Reagan. He was severely injured in an assassination attempt on the president, but remained the White House press secretary until the end of the administration. Since leaving the White House, Mr. Brady has lobbied for stronger gun laws. In November 1993, President Bill Clinton signed the Brady Bill, a national law requiring a waiting period on handgun purchases and a background check on buyers.